SOUTH
TO THE
POLE
BY SKI

Joseph E. Murphy

MARLOR PRESS

**Copyright 1990
by Joseph E. Murphy**

A Marlin Bree Book

SOUTH TO THE POLE BY SKI. Published by MARLOR
PRESS. All rights reserved. No part of this book may be published
in any form without the written permission of the publisher.

ISBN 943400-49-X

Distributed to the book trade by Contemporary Books Inc
180 North Michigan Avenue / Chicago, Illinois 60601
Telephone: (312) 783-9181

First Edition: 1990

Illustrations by Marlin Bree
Printed in the United States of America

Library of Congress Cataloging-in Publication Data

Murphy, Joseph E.
    South to the Pole by ski : nine men and two women pioneer a new route to the
South Pole / Joseph E. Murphy. -- 1st ed.
     p. cm.
    "A Marlin Bree book"--T.p. verso
    Includes index.
    ISBN 0-943400-49-X : $19.95
    1. South Pole. 2. Antarctic regions--Discovery and exploration.
I. Title.
G850 1988.M87 1990   90-6222
919.8'904--dc20   CIP

M A R L O R   P R E S S

4304 Brigadoon Drive / Saint Paul, Minnesota / 55126
Telephone (612) 484-4600

To Alejo, J.K., Jerry,
Jim, Martyn, Mike, Ron,
Shirley, Stuart, and Tori

Other books by the author:

*Adventure Beyond the Clouds: How We Climbed China's Highest Mountain and Survived**

With Interest: How to Profit from Interest Rate Fluctuations

Stock Market Probability: How to Improve the Odds of Making Better Investment Decisions

The Random Character of Interest Rates: Applying Statistical Probability to the Bond Markets

*This book won second prize from the Friends of American Writers

CONTENTS

MEMBERS OF THE EXPEDITION

Bajaj, J. K., *Member*
Age 46, married
Colonel, Indian Army,
Principal, Mountaineering School, Uttarkashi, U.P. India

Contreras-Steading, Alejo,
Representative of Chilean Government
Age 29, married
Guide, Santiago, Chile

Corr, Jerry, *Member*
Age 56, married
Real estate developer, Lansing, MI, U.S.A.

Hamilton, Stuart, *Snowmobile Operator*
Age 33, married
Hydrologist, Whitehorse, Yukon, Canada

Metz, Shirley, *Member*
Age 39, married
Retail consultant, Laguna Beach, CA., U.S.A.

Milnarik, Ronald, *Member*
Age 46, married
Colonel, U.S. Air Force. Endodontist
Belleville, Ill, U.S.A.

Murden, Tori (Victoria), *Member*
Age 25
Graduate Student, Harvard Divinity School
Louisville, KY, U.S.A.

Murphy, Joseph, *Member*
Age 58, married
Retired banker, writer, Minneapolis, MN, U.S.A.

Sharp, Mike, *Snowmobile Operator*
Age 37, Guide, Antarctica

Williams, Jim, *Assistant Leader*
Age 33, Guide,
Exum Guides, Jackson, WY, U.S.A.

Williams, Martyn, *Leader*
Age 39. Guide,
President, Adventure Network, Whitehorse, Yukon, Canada

SUPPORT STAFF

Campbell, Colin, *Pilot, DC-4*
Culver, Hugh, *Arrangements*
Adventure Network, Vancouver, B.C., Canada
Densmore, Lise, *Physician*
Whitehorse, Yukon, Canada
LeBon, Leo, *President*
Mountain Travel, Albany, CA, U.S.A.
LeBon, Nadia, *Arrangements*
Mountain Travel, Albany, CA, U.S.A.
Perk, Henry, *Pilot, Twin Otter*
Whitehorse, Yukon, Canada

APPLICANTS TO EXPEDITION

Beebe, Morton, *Photographer*
San Francisco, CA, U.S.A.
Senum, Reinette, *Actress*
Auburn, CA, U.S.A.
Wilson, Candace, *Store owner*
Toronto, Canada

OTHER PERSONS

Wiltsie, Gordon, *writer under contract to National Geographic*

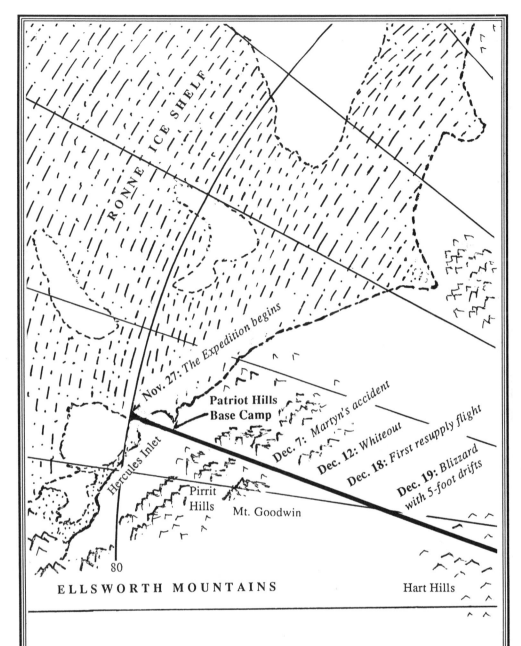

RONNE ICE SHELF

Nov. 27: The Expedition begins

Patriot Hills
Base Camp

Dec. 7: Martyn's accident

Dec. 12: Whiteout

Dec. 18: First resupply flight

Dec. 19: Blizzard
with 5-foot drifts

Hercules Inlet

Pirrit
Hills

Mt. Goodwin

80

ELLSWORTH MOUNTAINS

Hart Hills

To the South Pole by Ski

Highlights of the 750-mile South Pole
Overland Expedition, showing the team's progress

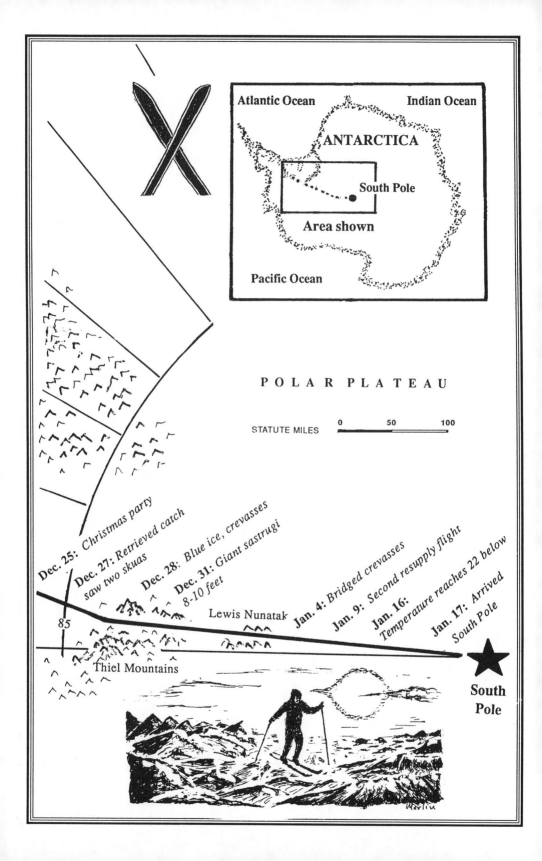

Atlantic Ocean   Indian Ocean

ANTARCTICA

South Pole

Area shown

Pacific Ocean

POLAR PLATEAU

STATUTE MILES   0   50   100

Dec. 25: Christmas party

Dec. 27: Retrieved catch saw two skuas

Dec. 28: Blue ice, crevasses

Dec. 31: Giant sastrugi 8-10 feet

Jan. 4: Bridged crevasses

Jan. 9: Second resupply flight

Jan. 16: Temperature reaches 22 below

Jan. 17: Arrived South Pole

85

Lewis Nunatak

Thiel Mountains

South Pole

PROLOGUE

ANTARCTICA, January 9, 1989: *85 degrees 20 minutes south latitude, 88 degrees 20 minutes west longitude, 390 miles south of the Patriot Hills, 322 statute miles north of the South Pole. Wind 10 m.p.h., temperature 8 degrees below zero Fahrenheit.*

THE TWIN OTTER hurriedly refueled at the remote gas cache in the Thiel mountains, then quickly took off again, heading on a course of 172 degrees to parallel the mountain range for 20 miles.

Then the airplane banked slightly right, passed King Peak off its left wing, and turned directly toward the South Pole.

The solitary search for the skiers had begun.

Dipping the wing slightly, the pilot now began scanning the horizon for the cairns. He hoped they would be visible at this hour in the low Antarctic light, when the sun was directly behind them.

In fact, he *had to find the cairns.*

These were the only markers to have been left by the nine men and two women who were boldly attempting the first crossing of this route by ski to the South Pole.

But the pilot saw only the sastrugi, the hard, wild frozen snow waves that twisted their way south. But it was too hard to leave a track from skis.

He glanced hopefully to his co-pilot. She shook her head.

Again, no cairns. *No sign of the missing skiers.*

Suddenly, he tensed. In the distance, he saw what he had not expected, but feared:

Deep cracks formed in the rough surface.

Crevasses!

These dark, dangerous chasms stretched south for miles in two long arcs.

Between the arcs, over the unknown depths, was only a narrow band of snow—a snowbridge.

As he stared in growing apprehension, the pilot was struck with a frightful new concern:

Could they not have seen the danger—and fallen through? Could the crevasse field have swallowed them up?

In the increasingly turbulent air, the Twin Otter shuddered. Below, the shadow of the small plane crept along the snow, moving unevenly over the hard surface.

But the pilot could see no sign of the expedition or their trail on the barren Antarctic snow.

They had been struggling for 42 days in the world's most inhospitable continent.

Now they were missing—alone at the end of the earth.

PREFACE

WE WERE SO DIFFERENT from each other.

There were the two women: one, a Harvard divinity student, was looking for God in the Antarctic; the other, a California blonde, had appeared in *Playboy*, wrote romantic poetry, and pursued fame.

Both wanted to go to the South Pole—though no woman had ever before succeeded in reaching it.

There were also the two colonels: the flamboyant Indian colonel with the black mustache who kept telling us we were doing it all wrong.

Sometimes, he was right.

His counterpart was the quiet American colonel, who often was too nice to disagree.

One of our expedition was a shopping-center developer, who trained by running up and down five flights of stairs with a pack on his back every day.

There were the guides: the American guide, who began climbing at 13, and the Chilean guide, who raced motorcycles and who limped from an accident in which he had lost a half inch of his leg.

The two Canadians were characters: one sometimes appeared at dinner on the trail in a bunny suit; the other, a Welshman, had yellow hair, told funny stories, and laughed a loud laugh.

Next, there was the wild-haired Englishman, who rode the snowmobile and had eyes for the woman from *Playboy*.

Lastly, there was the one who hardly ever trained and whom a Chilean newspaperman described as looking like a "mad professor."

And that was *me*.

In all, there were eleven of us. Together, we proposed to ski to the South Pole.

We planned, moreover, to do it on a route never done, never navigated, and never mapped.

We faced a number of obstacles before our journey even began. The trip would cost $400,000, a large sum, it seemed, but not for an expedition of this magnitude.

Moreover, no one was putting up corporate funds, or sponsorships, for us. We would have to pay for it all out of our own pockets.

We would be going against the initial wishes of the Chilean government, but its president later embraced us for our effort.

The U.S. government also objected to the trip and tried to pressure the Chilean government to stop us. The U.S. government's Antarctic expert told us the trip was too dangerous, hoping to discourage us, and issued misleading press releases saying that we relied on them for our safety.

Nonetheless, they treated us most graciously when the trip was over.

Danger was certainly a very real factor. The terror of the Antarctic has been long chronicled, reflected in the titles of the classic books about the continent: *Cold, Ice, The Worst Journey in the World.*

The statistics were grim: of the nine expeditions that attempted to reach the South Pole overland, three never advanced very far inland.

Of the *five* that made it that far, only *two* reached the pole overland by foot—and returned alive.

One other expedition got there, but all its members perished.

No *woman* had ever made it and no *American* had done it.

The dangers of the Antarctic have so frightened some commanders of the American stations that they would not allow their personnel to tread beyond the airstrip. To the American station personnel, the remainder of Antarctica apparently remains a dark, forbidden, and unknown continent.

That our party presumed not only to enter this world, but to cross half of it, seemed to them to court not only danger, but death.

In view of such foreboding, we might have been dissuaded. Here we were, preparing not only to go to this barren wasteland, but to cross 750 miles on foot. Was not this sheer arrogance? Or even unparalleled ignorance?

I must admit that I was not knowledgeable of many realities: what the land was like, what the dangers were, or even what my own abilities were, at age 58, to go that far by foot. Prior to contemplating the journey, I had never crossed the Arctic Circle; I had never been to the Antarctic, not even to Alaska.

Yet here I was, a retired banker telling myself that I was going to ski over the most treacherous piece of geography and in the worst climate on earth when the furthest I had ever skied was not much more than the three miles around the lake in front of my house.

Was I completely mad?

Some of my friends thought so.

Was I temporarily without reason? My wife thought so.

Was I trying to do something for which I had no training?

Everyone who knew me *knew* so.

Yet, the venture intrigued me. It caught my imagination for the very reasons that made it seem so illogical, so impossible.

First, it had been done only three times, because the terrain was so hard, so cold, so remote.

And second, it hadn't been done by anyone like me. People my age were supposed to take it easy and read or see movies about this kind of adventure.

Life was to be experienced vicariously while sitting in an armchair. That's what retired people are supposed to do.

I was not to think about something so extraordinary.

Certainly, I was not to try.

My mother, were she still alive, would have been aghast at such a venture. She had easily protected me from such foolishness when I was a child of five by tying me in a harness to a clothesline so I wouldn't wander out the yard and down the block.

Other relatives reminded me of my limitations.

"You're not a skier," one cousin said with a deeply worried look on her face.

"You're crazy to go. You know absolutely nothing about skiing."

She was only partly right: I did know something about cross-country skiing.

But I didn't know much: in fact, after a week of the training started, I broke my collarbone. This rather mercifully relieved me of any further need to undertake training, or even having to consider it.

Even my normally tolerant sons, who were used to such wild adventuring on their father's part, gave blank, somewhat skeptical looks when the trip was discussed.

I, of course, tried to keep the subject from ever coming up whenever my family or my friends were present.

When asked what I planned to do in the coming winter, I said simply that I planned to "do a little skiing down south."

That innocuous-sounding statement generally seemed to satisfy any curiosity of others.

Occasionally, there were further questions that every so often got me into trouble. They inevitably led to the dumfounded reaction, *"You're going to ski to the South Pole?"*

"Well, *yes*," I had to admit. "That's what I'm *thinking* of doing."

Then I would watch them shake their heads and walk off in a state of complete incredulity.

Section 1

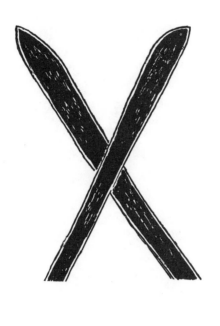

THE
EXPEDITION
BEGINS

1 / DECIDING TO GO

I WAS AT MY HOME in Minneapolis, seated in my gray leather chair before the fireplace of my den. The light shone brightly through the leaded glass windows off the white snow of Lake of the Isles. In the distance, I could see skiers on the trail around the lake. It was February, 1988, and cross-country skiing was in high season.

As I thumbed through the mail, the Mountain Travel catalog caught my eye. I turned to the catalog eagerly, putting aside the bills I would have to look at later, and thought of the trips I might take: a camel safari to Rajastan, trekking in New Guinea, a wildlife safari in South Africa. My mind relished the vision of these adventures.

But my musings over these trips were idle fantasies. I could not go to any of these places this year. Even so, I took pleasure in musing about the possibilities.

Then, unexpectedly, I noticed a description of an expedition to the *Antarctic*. I had long dreamed of exploring this remote and inhospitable continent.

A decade ago I had nearly gone, but my dream of being among the first to climb Antarctica's highest peak had vanished when the trip was canceled.

As I sat in my comfortable chair, I examined the details of the proposed expedition more carefully:

"The first international overland expedition to the South Pole by ski."

"No Americans have ever walked or skied to the South Pole," the catalog continued. *"No women have gone. If this expedition is successful, it will be the fourth to reach the Pole by foot, the first on a new route."*

I was fascinated by the prospect.

I recalled dreams I'd had as a teenager, when I cross-country skied on days when heavy blizzards had blocked all roads.

I would ski five miles to a neighborhood park in Minneapolis, moving in near silence through a sea of white. Only the faint sound of my wooden skis, schussing through the snow, could be heard. The buildings of the city, even the trees, were hidden from view by the quietly falling snow.

In this eerie world of white, I imagined that I was like Scott and Amundsen, making my way over the unexplored regions to the pole.

Intrigued, I read further about the expedition. *"The cost of this exceptional Mountain Travel tour is $69,500."*

The figure loomed starkly at me.

Most adventure trips cost *one-tenth* that amount. I had led *three* Himalayan mountain-climbing expeditions where the *total group cost* was less than the South Pole fee for *one* person.

My rambling thoughts of such a trip were idle, for I was already scheduled to lead a mountain-climbing expedition to Annapurna, a peak in the Himalayas, in the fall of 1989.

It would take two months, and that was enough time to be gone. Diana, my wife, would not tolerate another absence so soon.

My track record had not been too good. In the last eight years, I had been away on four expeditions—the first to India in 1980, when my best friend was killed; the last to Everest in 1986, when Diana did not hear whether I was alive or dead for three months.

I knew the South Pole expedition would be much harder on her than on me. It would be two months before she would know when I would return. I knew the worries and fears she would have: that I might be lost in a whiteout or devoured by a crevasse.

The cost of the trip was another drawback—nearly $70,000. That was more than my yearly salary when I worked at the bank five years before.

And so I decided against the trip. It was too much money to spend, too long to be away—absolutely impossible to consider.

I closed the catalog and put the thought of going on the Antarctic trip out of my mind.

A month passed. I took time out to helicopter-ski in the Caribous of Canada with a group of friends from Minneapolis. I tried to put aside thoughts of Antarctica, but they kept returning.

The appeal was too great to dismiss.

Soon I found I was turning over the advantages and disadvantages of the Antarctic expedition in my mind.

Certainly, the price was high, but in return I would have none of the problems of organizing an expedition myself.

I wouldn't have to worry about food, about getting the

equipment down to Antarctica, or about selecting a team.

Besides, I knew nothing about polar travel and would have to educate myself if I were going to organize an expedition myself. If I joined this expedition, Mountain Travel would take care of the organization.

Once again I sat back in my leather chair, glanced out the window at the snow, and mulled over the prospect.

A lot was attractive to me. I was nearly 58, my legs were in good shape, and I could walk and ski.

But in ten years, I would be too old for such a trip.

Not only that, there was room for only a limited number of skiers on the expedition. The trip might fill up; even now might be too late.

Moreover, this would be the only South Pole overland expedition; it was not to be repeated.

If I wanted to make the trip, I would have to act now. The longer I put it off, the less chance there would be of going.

Leo was reassuring on the telephone: "Yes, there is still room on the trip. No, you're not too old. In fact, I'm going. I'm your age. If you can stand 45 days in a sleeping bag, you can do it."

"You're going?"

"Yes! It will be a historic trip!"

Leo LeBon, the president of Mountain Travel, described briefly who had signed on.

First, there was Jerry Corr, an amateur sportsman who had climbed to 24,000 feet on the great Himalayan peak, Shisha Pangma. Good credentials—and Leo told me he was a friend of his. Another member, a Norwegian, had circumnavigated Norway by ski. Jim Williams, "his best guide," would also be along.

I'd first met Jim at an American Alpine Club dinner in New York several years ago, where he impressed me with his knowledge of Tibet. He had just returned from leading a trek to Bhutan. In the summer, he guided in the Grand Tetons. His ambition was to open his own guide service in Asia. Alert, hard-working, and observant, he could fix anything and talk about everything. I knew that he was competent and knowledgeable.

I was pleased to hear that Leo himself was going. Leo was 54, not much younger than I, and Jerry Corr was 57. Leo certainly didn't consider my age a problem.

My conversation with Leo came back to me again and again in the next few weeks. He had been very positive about the trip.

The group seemed to be experienced, one that would make a good expedition team.

And there was still room for me on the expedition.

Several weeks after the call to Leo, I reached in the bookcase for my checkbook, wrote out a check for the down payment. I put it in the Mountain Travel prepaid envelope, then set it out on the yellow wastebasket that served as our mailbox. The die was cast.

If I decided to back out, it would cost me the deposit. With that, I closed my mind on the matter.

I had paid, and I would go.

I still had to break the news to Diana at the appropriate time. The expedition was nearly a year off, so I figured there was no hurry. The important thing was that I had made the decision.

I conveniently forgot about the South Pole trip for the next couple of months, until a notice from California came in the mail.

The message was to the point: *"A training session will be held on Mount Rainier in June. Attendance is mandatory."*

Mandatory, I winced.

Although I didn't relish the idea of spending a week

on Mount Rainier, I reconciled myself to the idea. Attending a training session had advantages and one very decided disadvantage.

The primary advantage was that it would give me a chance to meet the leader, Martyn Williams, and the other members of the team. If I liked Martyn, and he seemed capable, then everything would be all right. If not, there could be problems.

The character and ability of the leader would be crucial to the success and enjoyment of the expedition. I also realized that if I were to spend two months with a group of people, I wanted to be certain they were people who would get along with each other—and with me. I knew that instinctively, and I knew it from personal experience from other expeditions.

The disadvantage of the training trip was that at last I would have to tell Diana about the expedition.

I knew she wouldn't like the idea, and I was concerned about how she might feel. I didn't relish bringing up the subject. But I knew I couldn't put it off any longer.

I waited until she was going off to a meeting in Chicago.

"I have to go to Mount Rainier in June," I said.

"To *where?*" she asked.

"Mount Rainier." I tried to make it sound as though it was the most natural place in the world to go.

"Whatever for?"

"It's a training trip!"

Diana looked perplexed. *"For what?"*

"The Antarctic trip!"

"Antarctic trip? *What Antarctic trip?"*

"I'm taking a ski trip in the Antarctic next winter."

She paused to let this sink in. *"How long will you be gone?"*

"Forty-five days."

As the details spilled out, Diana looked at me aghast.

"You'll be gone Thanksgiving, Christmas and New Year's—*all three holidays?*" she repeated, shocked.

"Yes," I admitted.

And so the plot was out. Later, the cost of the expedition came out, and that, too, was digested.

I do not like to think about decisions once they've been made. I decide, usually quickly, and then forget about the decision until I have to act.

This was the case with the Antarctic decision. Once I decided to go, I put the trip out of my mind.

My daily activities made that quite easy. I had little time left to think about, much less worry about, the Antarctic endeavor. It remained something that I was going to do in the future, not something I needed to consider actively right now.

Periodic correspondence from Mountain Travel jolted my calm anticipation. Actually these mailings were requests for prepayment.

Each time one came, I thought again and again about its implications: its cost, its length, and whether at my age I could do it.

Still, the decision had been made: I was going to go.

And there was, of course, the mandatory training on Mount Rainier. A lot would come into focus for me there.

2 / ON MOUNT RAINIER

THE MOUNT RAINIER LODGE was a log building with high ceilings, reminiscent of the great railroad structures of the national parks. I glanced about: the main hall was two stories high, with a circular balcony, and lined with photographs of the park's history.

I had already met several of the expedition members when I rode up the mountain with them in a rented car. Morton Beebe, a San Francisco photographer, had driven. Our skis and duffels containing sleeping bags, boots, and other gear were strapped on the roof. Jim Williams, a Mountain Travel guide, had been in the front passenger seat while I shivered in the back seat, feeling the cold seep through my jacket. Coming in June to Washington from warm Minnesota, I was not used to the cool temperatures of the high mountains.

We followed the winding road up Mount Rainier toward the lodge, watching the brown trees of the lowland give way to tall Douglas firs. Soon grass was replaced by snowbanks; the scenery turned white.

When we checked in at the front desk, I suggested to Morton that we share a room, and he readily accepted. Morton and I were about the same age, and though I didn't like the steady flow of talk, I felt comfortable with him. Jim Williams chose a single room, as he inevitably does, even though his boss, Leo LeBon, was always willing to double up.

The training meeting had been billed as mandatory. I was looking forward to seeing the other members of the expedition: to become acquainted with Martyn Williams, the leader of the expedition, and to get to know the other staff members.

In addition to training and meeting one another, we would also decide what equipment (personal equipment, as it turned out) was needed for the expedition. We would be briefed on communication procedures, practice ski navigation, and attempt some crevasse rescue techniques.

If we wished, we would have the opportunity to climb Mount Rainier, a chance I thought I wanted, since long ago I had tried unsuccessfully to climb that peak.

Though only 14,000 feet, Rainier could be difficult and dangerous because of its high winds and rapid weather changes. In a matter of hours, the peak could turn a gentle climb into a horrifying ascent.

It had claimed many lives, including that of Willie Unsoeld, the famed Everest climber. Not far from the hut near where we would be staying, he had been trapped in an avalanche and buried alive.

I was anxious to get to know our expedition leader. Martyn, I soon learned, was also president of Adventure Network International, which was the organizer of the expedition. In addition, he had extensive experience in the Antarctic, had opened up Mount Vinson to climbing expeditions, and had led a number of expeditions to that peak.

But climbing Mount Vinson was quite different from leading an expedition over an uncharted route to the South Pole. I was especially curious about what kind of person Martyn was, and whether I would like him as a friend and as the leader of the expedition.

These questions were foremost in my mind as I settled into the Mount Rainier Lodge. I realized that although I had made my initial deposit, I could still back out if I was not satisfied with either the leader or the team.

I also realized that the other members of the expedition were asking the same questions.

They wanted to discover who I was, too.

As team members in the Antarctic, we would depend on each other, perhaps for our lives.

Martyn was shorter than I, standing perhaps 5 feet, 8 inches, and wiry. Although he was only 40, his face was heavily lined. He had a great shock of yellow hair, which receded at the temples and on the crown, then sweeping out wildly in all directions.

Martyn talked in quick, staccato sentences, with a slight British accent—not an Oxford accent but something from the north. Welsh, red-faced, with a strong strain of Celtic blood, he was friendly and seemed to be very perceptive of others.

He had grown up in Great Britain. After college, he turned to Canada for work and adventure, becoming a teacher at the Ross Creek school for natives in the Yukon. Married and then divorced, he began organizing trips in the north of Canada and in Antarctica. Eventually, he helped to establish the first guided climbing trips to Mt. Vinson, the highest peak on the continent.

There was a wild side to Martyn, evidenced by his

unruly shock of yellow hair, loud laugh, and fine sense of irony.

Intellectually curious and quite reflective, he was a good story teller. He was not pretentious, and he had no interest whatsoever in the material things of life.

I discovered that climbing was his real love. To make this trip, his company, Adventure Network, had borrowed to the hilt. "I've never been in debt before," he said. "And I'm not sure I like the idea."

Martyn's assistant was Stuart Hamilton. Stuart grew up in Eastern Canada, attended the University of Alaska on a cross-country skiing scholarship, and then settled in the Yukon, where he worked for the government, measuring river flow. This work took him to remote parts of the province, usually on his own. I subsequently learned that Stuart liked to play practical jokes on the rest of us.

The notices from Mountain Travel had said there would be two women on the expedition. I was more than curious to meet them. But when I arrived at the lodge, I learned that there were not two but *four* women who wanted to go.

Not only that, but besides the guides, there were only *three* men, Jerry Corr, Morton Beebe, and me.

Jerry Corr was a real estate developer from Lansing, Michigan. He was a tough, wiry Irishman. Though he didn't say much, what he did say, he meant.

More important, he had a lot of high-altitude and expedition experience in the Himalayas and elsewhere. He had climbed Mount Vinson with Martyn. He had the cash and would definitely be on the trip.

Of the four women, only two had put down money: Shirley Metz, a retail chain-store owner from Southern California; and Victoria Murden, a Harvard divinity graduate student from Louisville, Kentucky.

Shirley was blonde with long, flowing hair and a trim, athletic figure. Her pretty face was tanned and her nose was slightly crooked in a way that made her seem even more attractive. Blue eyes peered at you in a straight forward manner.

She had spotted me first at the Seattle airport. "I'm Shirley Metz," she had said by way of introduction. She was standing in the bright sunlight near the car she had rented .

"*You* must be Joe Murphy—from *Minneapolis*."

I wondered how she knew. Shirley was wearing a fashionable outfit, not outlandish, but attractive and definitely California. And yes, I realized, this was the woman who once had been photographed in *Playboy* magazine.

"Why are you going on this trip to the South Pole, Joe?" she soon wanted to know.

"Because it's *there*," I replied, half in jest. It was the wrong answer to give her, I knew, even as I uttered it. Her slightly crooked nose seemed to twitch and her sleek eyebrows arched.

"Okay, then. Why are *you* going?" I countered.

"To promote a *world park*," she said. "To prevent pollution of the continent by industry."

A world park? I pondered that one.

Victoria Murden, or Tori, as she liked to be called, was quite different from California Shirley.

Tori had dark brown eyes and black hair which she wore in utilitarian fashion, straight down. She wore a look of determination.

She was tall, six feet, and though not slim, not overweight either. She looked to be strongly built.

I soon learned she was a very serious young woman. Considering her background, that probably was not unusual. Tori's family lived in Louisville, Kentucky, where her father taught classics. She was educated in a private school before finally going off to Smith College.

Tori had played varsity basketball at Smith and rowed on the crew. I was impressed when I learned she almost made it to the Olympics.

She had spent three months in Alaska with the National Outdoor Leadership School and two months in Africa, where she stalked lions and lived with the Masai. No stranger to hardship, Tori was not your ordinary 25-year-old woman.

No question about it: If either, or both, of these two strikingly different women should make it through the preliminary training, it would be a most interesting expedition.

And a very different one.

There were two other women who had applied. Both women were tough and likeable as potential team members, but it soon became apparent that neither had the funds to make the trip.

One was an actress, Reinette Senum, who, in her twenty-one years, had travelled around the world. Though she had a lot of adventures, she had little expedition experience. She was something of a comic, always ready to have fun, even at her own expense. She told me how she and her girlfriend had joined a nudist colony in their travels through Greece and had undressed like the others to avoid being conspicuous. Reinette made no pretense of having skied before.

The fourth woman was an athletic type, a helicopter pilot from Toronto who had trained with the Canadian national downhill team. Her name was Candace Wilson. She was 34, single, had studied archaeology in Paris, and now made and sold men's clothing on order.

That left us with one member yet unaccounted for: Ron Milnarik, a strong candidate, but unable to come to Rainier. A U.S. Air Force colonel, he needed all his leave for the expedition. So he had none to spare for the training.

After supper the first night, we met for the first time as a group to go over equipment and plans. But the meeting got started late since not everyone arrived on time. Martyn surprised us by asking each of us why we wished to join the expedition.

"I want to create a world park," Shirley said, continuing her concept, "to preserve that part of the world from pollution."

"I was in Antarctica last year," she said, "on the *Discovery*. I made a film of the event. It was shown on Public Television."

Shirley looked around intensely. Clearly she had prepared in advance what she wanted to say, with rebuttal if necessary. No one questioned her.

When Shirley finished, the rest of the group gave brief talks. *Why were we going on this trip?*

It was a good question, but hard to answer. We all knew we had volunteered to endure harsh conditions, spending two months in the coldest continent in the world, sleeping on the ice, and skiing eight or nine hours a day. And we were paying to do it.

When my turn came to answer, I struggled for a moment to collect my thoughts.

"Because it's a *historic trip*," I finally said. "Because no Americans have skied to the South Pole. I guess I want to see if I can do it."

As I uttered these phrases, I knew they sounded slightly cliche. But I felt they were important parts of my reason for going. In truth I realized my personal decision was complex and I did not fully understand why I wanted to go.

Partly it was a personal challenge. For us, on this trip, there would be a lot of hardships and probably no glory. Certainly, there would be none if we failed to reach the pole. That was a real possibility. But just trying would be a grand adventure.

To my surprise, I found that others answered Martyn's question along somewhat the same lines: It was a historic trip and there was new ground to be explored.

When Victoria Murden's turn came, she had a different reason. "As you know, I'm a divinity student," she said, with a wry smile. "And I'd like to see what it's like when Hell freezes over."

We all laughed, especially Tori. She had a loud, boisterous laugh. She also enjoyed her own jokes.

"Seriously, though," she continued, "this is part of my thesis topic for my Master's Degree—on the spiritual aspect of adventure."

I wondered if the thesis was the excuse, not the real reason, for her coming.

It became clear that all of us were investing heavily in the expedition. Tori was depending on her grandmother's inheritance; Shirley, on her brother's bequest; Jerry, on another loan from the bank, the bank that financed his shopping centers; and I, on funds acquired recently from a family company.

Martyn also was spending large sums to make the expedition possible, with three years of work and a large loan to finance the DC-4 and Twin Otter aircraft already contracted. If this expedition did not go, Martyn would lose heavily both in time and money.

As we talked, Martyn's gray eyes betrayed no reaction to what each of us had said in response to his question. But I could see that he was evaluating our responses and testing our resolve to go to the pole.

He had cause for concern. Whether we went, and whether we would make it, depended on our own individual determination. None of us were hardened, professional athletes; we were all amateurs from different walks of life.

Martyn could not force us to ski 750 miles across the barren continent. He could only facilitate the trip and provide the logistics—the planes, the food, and the shelter.

The execution of the plan over the long pull would require each of our individual effort, personal strength and will.

Once again, I wondered if we could do it.

This was turning out to be perhaps an all-time unique expedition to the pole. Martyn was not in a position to pick a team of the best or strongest skiers he could find. Instead, he had to depend on those who came through the mail from Leo LeBon's adventure travel company, Mountain Travel.

Actually, Martyn had no control. Though our polar leader, he was totally unlike the early arctic explorers, Scott, Amundsen, and Shackleton, who had secured their own funding and then carefully screened the best men for the trip.

Martyn had to depend upon getting volunteers who were not only determined enough to attempt the trip and who could pay their own way. Like a fisherman who takes a chance on what's in the stream, Martyn could only put out the bait and hope for a good catch. He could not control what he took in.

I sensed some tension in the room at this first meeting. We all knew that Martyn depended on us and that we depended on him —that the organization and financing were parts of the same equation. Without either, the enterprise would fail.

This implicit mutual dependence was never voiced or stated as such, but we all felt it and knew it was there.

For the expedition to go, we needed a minimum of six members. So far, only *five* had made down payments: Jerry, Tori, Shirley, Ron, and me. Morton, Candace, and Reinette had not yet put down a cent.

We needed one more person to finance the expedition.

So, to the boldness and dangers of the polar quest was added the uncertainty of the expedition's even getting off the ground. There were many reasons for the tension in the air.

After everyone had spoken, Martyn thanked us. But he now seemed to have something else on his mind.

Still showing no emotion or offering comment, he continued in a dead-pan manner: "And now my assistant will demonstrate an essential piece of equipment."

Stuart slowly crossed the room, reached behind a chair, and pulled out a strange-looking piece of gear. We all wondered what came next as he held up a leather-studded collar with a locking piece at the bottom.

I could see that it was about the size of the neck of a large dog or maybe even a wolf, and it was strongly constructed. Maybe it was *a dog collar.*

At the bottom hung a dull metal object, a two-inch cube with a slender six-inch wire hanging down.

"This," carefully explained Stuart, "is to be worn by *all members* of the expedition."

We were startled as Stuart opened the collar, placed it over his head, drew it down on his neck—then snapped the lock.

"You can see how it fits." Stuart helpfully continued: "Each collar contains a radio with a unique signal so we can locate you in the event you fall down a crevasse or get lost."

Shirley's eyes now opened wide in wonderment.

But Stuart continued with a perfectly straight face, objectively explaining the intricacies of the radio:

"Each Ski-Doo," he said "will have a receiver."

He looked around, as if for emphasis.

Some of the expedition members seemed horror-struck that their leader was suggesting he or she wear a dog collar. No matter for what purpose.

Shirley looked as if she was about to say something when, suddenly, Martyn blurted out: "It's a *wolf collar*—the kind used to track wolves." Then he let out a deep, loud laugh.

Martyn quickly explained the device was a put-on—all but the transmitter. We would each carry a transmitter in a small silver box, but not a leather collar.

As Martyn laughed again, we joined in. Those who had not caught the joke at the beginning uttered a sigh of relief.

But we all realized we would be in the company of humorists and pranksters for the expedition.

"Too late to finish the rest of our business," Martyn concluded. "We'll meet tomorrow morning at 8:00 a.m. to finish up the plans. Then, we'll go skiing."

I returned to my room. My body felt tired after the long flight and ride up to the lodge. I was not absolutely certain of the people who would make up the expedition, or, in fact, if there would be an expedition.

I could feel a draft of cold air when I opened the window of our room. The fog from outside slowly drifted in, bringing a damp chill with it. I was glad to crawl beneath the woolen blankets

The next morning, clouds covered the slopes surrounding the mountain lodge. I feared we would not be able to train or to ski, due to dense fog that pervaded everything around us. I reported for the meeting, anxious about what we'd do.

Hugh Culver, the administrative chief of Adventure Network, began by passing out thick brochures that contained detailed information on the expedition. I glanced through the pages and saw sections on navigation, history, air support, conditions in the Antarctic, and, at the end, an equipment list. I recalled that we had been sent a booklet on Antarctic survival, information I had found interesting and helpful.

Martyn opened the meeting with a discussion of communications.

"We'll have radio communications with base camp in the Patriot Hills and with our base in Punta Arenas at all times," he emphasized. "We will also have contact by satellite with the international station in Paris, and will send our location and temperature to Paris twice a day. Paris, in turn, will relay the information to Vancouver, and Vancouver will send it on to Mountain Travel in Albany, California."

After this reassuring news, which meant that Diana could be kept informed of my progress, Martyn proceeded with the equipment list.

It was detailed: polypropylene long underwear, pile jacket and pants, windshell pants and jacket, down jacket and down pants for extremely cold weather, two pairs of cross-country ski boots with insulated overboots or gaiters, pile mitts with shells, glacier goggles, and pile hat.

"We will purchase the boots, skis, and poles," said Martyn. "We will also get the Canadian military boots—for extreme cold."

It was standard mountaineering equipment, most of which I had. But we discussed all getting the same equipment through a single supplier.

Martyn felt that getting uniform equipment was important. "So we can be sure it's right." I agreed. He suggested a supplier, and we agreed to go along with the purchase.

The expected cost was $600 each, after the expedition discount of 40 percent or more.

Following the equipment meeting, Leo asked for a separate meeting of the four who had made deposit. The four were: Tori, Jerry, Shirley and I. As we assembled, I wondered exactly what Leo wished to discuss.

He came right to the point: "The expedition will cost $400,000. We have guaranteed Adventure Network this amount. I don't know whether that figure gives them a profit or not."

Leo looked a little worried. "We are still short one person. Morton is a possibility, but the odds seem low. Reinette is enthusiastic, but she has raised no funds to date. Candace is a possibility. Ron Milnarik will be coming, even though he isn't here for the training. There is also a remote possibility that an Indian colonel may join the party. Finally, a Norwegian who circumnavigated his country by ski may come. He is definitely interested, but his coming hinges on working out a sailing expedition with Mountain Travel using his boat."

He paused, then asked the critical question: Whether we wanted to go badly enough to make up the difference if a sixth person could not be found.

It would mean we'd each have to put up another $10,000.

Both Jerry and I said we definitely would.

Shirley was still game. "The trip is costing me $100,000 anyway."

The reported cost was $69,500, excluding training and equipment. I wondered where Shirley got her figure.

Tori wasn't sure where she would get the money.

Leo reiterated that he was losing money on the project. He'd already spent more than $20,000, his total expected commission. He had numerous expenses. He, his wife Nadia, and Jim Williams were all at Mount Rainier working on the arrangements. That meant costs of airfare, car, fuel, and hotel.

Finally, we agreed to share the extra cost—if we had to. Once again, the trip was on.

Our decisions made, we trekked out of the small meeting room and reassembled a short time later in the large log structure of the Mount Rainier lodge. Time for training.

"A new outfit!" I said to Shirley. She had changed into a new, colorful ski suit. Martyn wore his old green pants. Tori was in her gray Patagonia pants. Of the men, only Stuart looked trim in his flashy spandex cross-country tights. We were a sight to behold—two of us very chic, the rest a little dowdy.

We had been told we would use skis to climb part way up the mountain. I had gone to my room to get my Fisher Europa Mountain skis and brand new skins (strips of cloth, smooth on one side and furry on the other, that attach to the bottom of skis to climb steep hills).

I was a little worried: I hadn't used skins for 30 years and the old ones I was used to were quite different from these. Carefully, I clamped the rubber bands of the skins over the tip of the skis and then gradually smoothed the skins to the skis. I followed the instructions, but the bottom of the skin kept coming loose. Stuart showed me how to adjust the top so that the bottom end would fit perfectly.

Beyond the asphalt parking lot, a 20-foot bank of snow rose in the mist. Beyond, rose the flanks of the mountain.

We set off up the mountain on our skis at a good clip, with Martyn in the lead. Our skins gave traction in the wet snow. I felt the snowflakes falling on my neck and shoulders, and I shivered in the cold.

Slowly, we traversed the mountain's lower slope. Then we turned up a steep pitch. My skins held, and slowly, we gained altitude.

"Don't lift your skis from the snow," Stuart instructed. Having cross-country skied since I was 10, I knew what he was talking about. I knew you were supposed to keep your skis flat, to slide them. But knowing and doing were two different things.

And here I was, getting used to cross-country skiing again after not having done it for a while.

We climbed for two hours, and then we descended.

I'll keep the skins on during the descent, I thought, since that would slow my speed. It worked quite well.

Martyn and Stuart telemarked gracefully down the slope in the mist, while the rest of us plodded our way down.

Over the succeeding days, we practiced climbing on skins, traversing, and descending, and finally, finding direction in dense fog by compass.

To move by compass, you looped the string of the instrument around your neck, and then held the compass in your right hand, level with your eyes. After you set the bearing, you aimed the compass in the direction you wanted to go, and picked out a landmark in that direction.

Once you had the landmark selected, you headed out directly toward it. The lead person chose the direction, and the others followed in single file.

"Whiteout will be a problem in the Antarctic," predicted Martyn. "We'll have to learn to travel in a straight line with an accurate compass bearing."

We worked on other techniques. In one, the last skier told the lead skier to move left or right when he veered from the line of skiers, which meant he was off course. We also practiced making adjustments for magnetic declination.

The next morning, we set off, the ten of us: Martyn, Stuart, Jim, Shirley, Tori, Reinette, Candace, Jerry, Morton, and I. A light snow fell from the cloudy sky. We camped in a saddle just to the east of the main summit of the mountain. It was about a hundred yards behind the huts used by the Rainier mountain guides.

The wind was blowing hard, building the snow into drifts. Time for us to try out our tents.

We pulled three North Face tents out of their stuff sacks, thrust the long fiber poles into the circular sleeves, and pushed the yellow domes up against the wind. They went up quickly, billowing in the gusts.

I was glad. My down jacket was soaked from the last hour, and I regretted not having brought my pile jacket. A wet down jacket is useless against the cold. Unless the jacket dried, I could freeze.

Martyn had assigned Candace and me to one tent and the rest of our group to the two other tents, which had been pulled together to form a long house that was to serve as a mess and cook tent.

After quickly arranging my air mattress and sleeping bag, I crawled out into the cold to get to the mess tent for dinner. Here I could dry my jacket and get a preview of tomorrow's activities.

We learned we would be heading for the crevasses.

"Have you ever fallen down a crevasse?" I asked Candace.

"No," she replied. *"Have you?"*

I shook my head. It was not something I even wanted to think about.

The next morning when we reached the crevasses, we laid out the ropes across the snow and then moved in threes up to the open fissures in the glacier.

Plucky Reinette was first to jump into the crevasse. After being roped up, the technique was simple: you just screwed up your courage—and jumped.

As soon as I felt the jerk from her fall, I fell backwards, digging my heels into the snow.

She disappeared over the edge.

When the motion stopped, I jammed the staff of my ice axe into the snow nearly up to the blade, then secured the rope to it with a prussik line and carabiner.

"Are you all right?" I called down.

"Fine!" she replied, bravely. Reinette was sitting in her body harness, looking extremely uncomfortable.

Then we pulled her back up. One by one we all tried
crevasse jumping. And dangling in the icy abyss.

I wondered whether we would actually be endangered
by crevasses in the Antarctic. I was familiar with the
dangers of crevasses in the mountains, but I had never
fallen into one.

I hoped we would not have to ski roped up, since the
ropes would slow us down greatly. Even walking roped
up is very cumbersome. But I knew the ropes would be
a safeguard against crevasses.

The next day, we practiced ice climbing rather
uneventfully. As the sun set beyond Rainier's upper
slopes in the west, we headed back up the slope on our
skis and skins.

The slope looked innocent now in the afternoon sun,
until someone pointed out the very place where the
famed Everest climber Willie Unsoeld had died in an
avalanche. Once again, I reminded myself not to take
the mountains too casually.

The following day, there was too much fog for
climbing, so we practiced more crevasse rescue before
heading back to the lodge.

Though we had gotten through all of the toughest
parts of our training without injury, it seemed almost
ironic that on the way down, Shirley badly twisted her
ankle.

She didn't discover the full extent of the damage until
she returned to California. The injury would keep her in
a brace for the next several months.

It could ruin her opportunity to go to the pole—and
perhaps even affect the chances of the team.

On the way out, Martyn pulled into the Rainier Park
headquarters to inspect a prototype of the mess-and-
cook tent he planned to use in the Antarctic.

His humor came to the fore again. He playfully named

it the "Transportable Utility Retractable Dome," and I wondered why he had done that.

Then he told me that it was the *"TURD"* for short.

The name, of course, stuck.

On my flight home, I considered our parting instructions from Stuart, which had been to train *actively*. We were told to walk, run, paddle, and, if possible, roller-ski.

"It's *essential*," he explained patiently to all us amateur polar explorers, "to train *properly* if you want to complete the journey."

I don't like training, and I'd planned mostly to forget about the Antarctic trip until the next session, which was scheduled for the fall.

But the necessity of making a minimum effort to train was clear. I had to do *something*.

In desperation, I purchased a pair of roller skis and began to use them. A week later, I had a bad fall and had my collarbone x-rayed.

"It's broken," the doctor confirmed.

"But I'm planning to ski to the South Pole in November."

"Ski *where*?" he asked incredulously.

"To the *South Pole*."

He paused, a quizzical look on his face.

"You'll be out of this in a month," he said, but warned me, *"no exercise this summer!"*

That emphatically finished my training for a while.

I'd just have to go to the last training session with no practice.

3 / NORTH TO
THE YUKON

BY THE END OF THE SUMMER, my collarbone was well on the way to healing. There was a large bump, to be sure, and the two bones were slightly offset, but not badly. My doctor had given me reluctant permission to travel north to the Yukon.

But when it was time to leave in September, 1988, I was not anxious to go. We had already had one session and I didn't see why two were necessary.

Besides, getting to Whitehorse from Minneapolis was not cheap. I had to fly to Chicago, backtrack to Vancouver, then fly on up to Whitehorse in the Yukon. The return flight routed me back through Salt Lake.

I booked the flight, packed my belongings—skis, boots, and sleeping bag—and prepared for the trip.

I didn't quite trust Martyn to get a proper fit on my boots. It was hard enough for me to do that at home, since I'd had a quadruple-E foot before four toes had been amputated after a mountaineering accident in the Himalayas 30 years ago.

Despite a missing big toe, my right foot was still too wide for most boots. It was rare that I found a proper fit.

When I checked through Canadian customs and found the check-out point for Whitehorse at a far corner of the Vancouver airport, I noticed an Indian sitting on the bench across from me. His body was erect with the definite bearing of a military officer.

I wondered if it was J. K. Bajaj, the Indian who might accompany us. He would be the sixth and final member of the expedition unless, of course, Leo had found others. After weighing the possibilities that the distinguished figure might be a member of our expedition, I asked him if he was going to meet Leo LeBon.

"I am," he replied. "Are you also one of the members of the South Pole expedition?"

Within minutes, we became acquainted. We shared a row of seats on the half-empty plane headed for Whitehorse. J. K. filled me in on his background, and I said that I had visited his homeland. I perceived him as a charming individual, and I was immediately glad he was going. He would add to the variety of the expedition members. My fears of the difficulty of an Indian were relieved; he might turn out to be difficult, I thought, but he certainly is charming.

It was getting dark by the time we took off, but I still could see the white peaks of the Coast Range in the fading light of the sun from the west.

The Coast Range was nearly as untracked as it was

when I had been there a quarter century ago. It was an enormous, uncharted blank on the map.

Its remoteness now reminded me of our destination, the Antarctic. We were going to another blank on the map, much more remote, largely uncharted, and far more difficult to reach than the mountains below us.

As the plane descended to the airport, my mind ran over the impending training and expedition. Was I crazy to be doing this? I was nearly 60 years old, and I was attempting to do something which only eight people had ever done and lived. Moreover, they were considerably younger than I when they had done it.

We were booked to stay in the Gold Rush Hotel on the main street of Whitehorse. The main street wasn't much, six or eight blocks of assorted hotels, stores, and gas stations. The heyday of this town, the gold rush at Dawson Creek, had been long ago. Now it was turning into an outdoor and sports center as well as remaining a mining town.

The Gold Rush Hotel was clean and comfortable, and the restaurant was a hangout for local citizens. I suggested to J. K. that we share a room, and he agreed.

Most of the other potential members of the expedition were already there, Jerry, Shirley, Reinette, Tori, but not Candace. She had apparently dropped out. Ron had not yet arrived, but would come on Friday with Leo. All guides were there, Martyn, Jim, and Stuart.

The expedition was being assembled. Tomorrow we would train.

A gray sky hung over the broad valley of the Yukon, which ran by Whitehorse. The sun was occluded, and the effect was somber.

Because of the overcast, we would have to find another area to ski in. Martyn was soon on the phone. But there was no snow here in the valley or even a little higher up. But there might be a snow-covered glacier further away.

While he checked, we assembled at the Whitehorse Outdoor Center, which had been built for the training of Canadian Olympic cross-country skiers. Our trainers, who also were part of the Olympic training, had volunteered their time for us. We would train on roller skis.

J. K., who had never skied and never skated, worked doggedly at his strides, while Shirley, despite her ankle splint, strode resolutely up and down in the morning mist.

For our efforts, Stuart gave us periodic encouragement. He also supervised the warming-up exercises at the end of the roller-ski demonstration. He suggested we use these exercises when we got to the Antarctic.

Martyn saved the day. He had located some appropriate snow.

We would drive to Skagway, Alaska, where we would be flown by helicopter up to a snow-covered glacier.

The border was not far, so we drove in Martyn's van; we cleared customs and arrived at Skagway shortly after lunch.

The helicopter pad was located between the town and the harbor along the main street. The helicopters were used primarily to take tourists up for a view of the glacier above the town.

We gathered our camping gear and skis and headed for the takeoff pad.

As the blast of cold air swept past me, I watched the small helicopter lift off, angle forward, and head toward the glacier. It carried our food, tents, and skis. The glacier was 2,000 feet above us and just below an unnamed peak of the Coast Range of Alaska.

By the time it was my turn, the clouds had begun to settle in. We climbed 2,000 feet and headed across the glacier. As we came in, I saw the mess tent erected in the snow and surrounded by a line of skiers and boxes of food.

When we landed, I climbed out, ducked below the blades, and headed toward the tents. The others were all there; only Jim remained to be brought up from below.

Although we had passed a heavy crevasse area at the bend in the glacier, the camp site was uncrevassed, flat, and covered with two feet of snow. A light breeze wafted over the snow as the sun began settling in the west.

We had arrived late and would be late setting up. Martyn's girlfriend had joined us and made dinner in the mess tent where we assembled after our own tents were up.

We spent the night in tents on the glacier.

It was cold and clear the next morning when we resumed our training under the watchful and determined eyes of Stuart. He first described the strides and then demonstrated them, one by one.

"Kick, kick," he barked. "You're not getting the proper glide."

The drills continued endlessly.

We skied with poles, without poles, in tracks, outside tracks, and back and forth until we were completely exhausted. By the end of the next day, we had worked up from the diagonal stride to full skating.

It was not always easy, particularly for me after years of bad form. I found only the skating easy—since I'd often skated on my downhill skis.

We ended each day with a three-kilometer run in a quiet circle around the snow of the glacier.

Then, in our tired state, we watched televised shots of our efforts. I could see I needed improvement. My legs and arms moved much more slowly than I had thought, and my skiing form looked much worse that I had imagined.

In truth, I looked like a huge bear, slowly lumbering

across the snow. I was not the graceful athlete I had imagined myself to be in my romantic dreams.

We were physically tired, but the discussion of equipment back at the tent didn't turn out to be too restful.

"Our supplier didn't work out," Jim said. "But we've gotten a 50 percent discount from Marmot. We'd like all of you to get Marmot gear, if you're willing."

I really didn't need any more equipment, I had so much already. But I had agreed earlier to buy the common equipment, so I said yes. Except for Shirley, the others did, too.

"I have a contract with North Face," Shirley announced. "The 50 percent discount isn't enough. I can get better than that at my store. I'll be wearing North Face—specially designed for me."

She would probably be the most stylish polar explorer ever, I realized.

But Shirley not only seemed angry at Jim and Leo for intimating that she should be buying the Marmot gear, but something else that involved several of the team.

Shirley snapped, "I'd like to discuss a philosophical point."

Shirley twisted in her chair as she spoke and looked quite agitated. Obviously she had something on her mind.

"Tori will speak first," Shirley announced.

Tori also was agitated. She began by saying that she had thought that this was an expedition, "not a tour."

"I'm not going to spend $70,000 for a tourist trip," she protested. "I was ready to cry when I heard Jim describe it as a tour. I thought it was an *expedition*—not a *tour*! I'd rather give the money to the needy. If it's just a commercial tour, I don't want to go!"

Reinette started to say something when Shirley

snapped tersely, "Cool it! Tori is talking." Shirley was normally very controlled. The outburst was unusual.

There seemed to be something more going on than I knew of or suspected. We obviously had to settle the matter of the terminology for everyone's benefit, but suddenly I heard a roar outside, the familiar sound of helicopter blades.

Saved by the chopper.

"It's Leo and Ron," someone said.

Ron was dressed in wool knickers, long socks, a wind parka, and wool ski cap. He seemed quiet and nice.

Not long after landing, Leo came up to me and asked, "Are you still on?"

"Of course," I replied. "I wouldn't miss it." The expedition was turning out to be very interesting. I hoped, however, not too interesting, judging from the outbursts earlier.

And I wondered why he had asked.

The answer was not long in coming. After we reassembled in the tent, Leo came right to the point:

"The expedition will cost $400,000. So far, we have only $350,000 and only five members. J. K. wants to go, but as of this date he has paid no money. Only five have made deposits, and only Shirley is fully paid."

"I will send you a check for the balance as soon as I get home," I promised.

The others made similar commitments.

But there were other problems. Leo had met with the National Science Foundation. They didn't want us to go. What was worse, the U.S. government was putting severe pressure on the Chilean government not to allow us to fly.

Moreover, Adventure Network had borrowed large sums. If there was an accident, the monies paid and due would not cover it.

The National Science Foundation didn't want us to be

there because they didn't want the responsibility of rescuing us. And they didn't have the equipment to do it. If someone sued Mountain Travel or Adventure Network, that would not be covered either. There were a lot of risks.

I turned aside to ask Jerry why Leo had said all this.

"He just wanted us to know what the risks are." Jerry also suspected that Leo might be trying to back out.

When Leo finished, J. K. reported that he had to get permission from the Bank of India to take funds out of India, which was to conform to Indian currency regulation.

As a military officer, he needed permission from the Minister of Defense to go on the expedition. He required authorization of his superior and the Mountaineering Federation to go, and he had to get the permission of the Minister of Foreign Affairs. Securing these permissions was not easy.

Leo said that he understood and that he knew J. K. would come through.

With that, the meeting ended. We looked at the television shots of our skiing. It was apparent that our skiing had improved considerably, but we all knew Leo was at his diplomatic best when he said he was impressed.

Each day but the last was clear. The sun penetrated to our opening on the glacier, bringing warm, glistening brightness.

On the last day, the clouds moved in. We feared that we might have to ski out, or worse, hike out. That would be a long, hard descent, one I did not relish, for Skagway was several thousand feet below.

To avoid having to hike out, Martyn cut the last day short, called in the helicopters, and suggested we strike the tents and pack our gear for departing.

Soon, the small machine wheeled in below the clouds,

lowered itself to the landing area, and, with a roar, put its skis on the ground. The cloud bank was drifting east toward the mountains, and the small gap in the clouds narrowed and began to endanger our escape.

When my turn finally came to climb aboard, the helicopter edged up through the narrow gap in the clouds, and then slipped down to the fjord and Skagway.

I felt much relieved that we did not have to hike out.

Our adventure was over. But I didn't realize what a close call we had until I later learned that after the last skier left, the clouds had closed in. It was a week before the chopper was able to retrieve the mess tent and the rest of our camping gear.

As we waited back in town, the sun played upon the landing. I could see the large tourist boat off in the harbor.

An elderly couple passed us and asked where we had been.

"On the glacier above," I replied, "skiing."

They looked back at the awesome mountains so far away, capped with clouds. I wasn't sure they believed me.

We returned to Whitehorse the way we had come, crossing through customs. Before leaving, Martyn issued telemark boots and Canadian military boots to most of us. The next morning, we prepared to depart from Whitehorse and return to our various homes.

We had spent only a week here—and we already were beginning to have problems as a team.

I learned that after only two days Shirley had refused to stay in her assigned tent because she couldn't get along with one of the women.

I wondered: What would she be like on an expedition

which lasted two months? What would she do if she couldn't get along with one of us?

It was not a comforting question.

The training ended, we all went our separate ways. I took the plane back with Ron, who was headed for St. Louis via Salt Lake.

I was just getting to know him. He told me one anecdote about himself that stuck in my mind:

"My commander was supposed to run a 100-kilometer race in Germany," he said, "but couldn't. So he asked if I wanted to take his slot. Though I had never run before, I said I would. I ran 80 kilometers. But then I had to quit—in fact, I could no longer stand up."

I laughed at the story and told him I certainly wouldn't start out long-distance running by attempting a 100-kilometer marathon. As I reflected later on Ron's story, I came to notice the iron determination that was hidden beneath his quiet manner.

Ron, I learned on the flight, had skied a million vertical feet in the Bugaboos. So he was no beginner on skis.

One less problem to worry about.

But as I relaxed on the flight back to Minneapolis, other questions continued to bombard my mind:

What was Shirley really like?

Would J. K. actually raise the money? Did Leo want to back out of the trip?

Would Martyn get permission from the Chileans to fly from Punta Arenas to his base camp in the Antarctic?

How much would I have to train? Would I be strong enough to do the trip? So far, my collarbone had healed enough to allow me to cross-country ski.

When I reached home, Diana was delighted to see me.

She didn't like the idea of the South Pole trip in the

first place, but to have me home from Alaska was a relief.

"You'll be gone for *two months* and *three holidays*," she still lamented.

"Well, perhaps not Thanksgiving," I only could say in my own defense.

Section 2

THE
FIRST STEPS
TO THE POLE

4 / SOUTH TO CHILE

As IT TURNED OUT, I would be gone on
Thanksgiving, too. The initial schedule had us leaving
November 25—the day before Thanksgiving. After
some complaints, the departure date was moved to the
day after Thanksgiving.

But when the airline tickets came, the 25th remained
the departure date as originally scheduled. We were to
return the 25th of January, a full two months later. I
didn't relish telling Diana this news.

"Forty-five days of skiing," the original schedule had
said. I stuck to that number in my mind and in talking
to others. The schedule was tight.

If we didn't get to the South Pole by the first week of
February, it would be too cold to land the airplane. So
the scheduled return of January 25 was more or less an
outside guess.

The weeks slipped by gradually, and the polar expedition was still a long way off. From time to time, I worked on getting my equipment together.

Each year there seemed to be better equipment. Indeed, there were improvements. Polypropylene was better than wool, and Capilene was better than the original polypropylene; it didn't smell, and it didn't turn oily.

Although we had been advised to take Helly-Hansen underwear, and most did, I stuck to Patagonia's Capilene, which I knew from experience worked well.

The Marmot gear had been ordered, but I preferred Moonstone equipment. I had also ordered a heavy jacket and a one-piece suit from Wild Things that had been used by Will Steger on his North Pole and Greenland expeditions, trips that were good tests of the gear.

A one-piece suit kept you extremely warm, and this suit was Gortex, lightly insulated with Hollofil. It was light, absorbed perspiration, and did not bind in the arms, shoulders, or legs. It had an oversized knee for easy leg action, a hood, and a half-moon rear double zipper for going to the bathroom. It seemed perfect in every respect.

The Hollofil jacket was large, hooded, and had more insulation than I'd seen in any other jacket. It was an improvement over the parkas I had used on earlier expeditions. I had ordered the suit and jacket in time to test them in Alaska, and they had worked very well.

The remaining equipment was largely supplemental. Jim had ordered from Marmot a pile jacket and pants, an insulated bib, down jacket, and pants; a pile hat, and a shell jacket and pants.

We were also instructed to buy an extra lightweight shell from Marmot. The clothes were red and black, good for being spotted in the snow in a storm, but not at all attractive. I certainly wouldn't wear them anywhere else. The safety of red, I felt, was more important than the looks.

No one had taken our intended route to the South Pole before. Thus, the way was unknown and largely unexplored.

Perhaps for these reasons, Jim was overly cautious, asking us to take much more than we actually needed. As a result, everyone but Shirley chose Marmot gear.

The books on weather survival strongly recommended vapor-barrier liners for feet, legs, body and sleeping bag.

Will Steger, the North Pole explorer, also endorsed this view when I talked with him. But I suspected the theories were wrong, for the Antarctic is very dry. I ultimately discarded all vapor barriers except boot and sleeping-bag liners.

I worried about another problem instead: the weight of the emergency equipment the skiers were to carry and how they were to carry it.

I didn't want to haul a lot of gear on skis, particularly not on my back.

In Whitehorse, Jim had announced on the last night that he and Martyn had weighed the emergency personal gear each of us would carry.

"It comes to 35 pounds," he said.

"How *can it*?" I asked, incredulously.

"I'm not going to carry thirty-five pounds to the pole," I argued. "That's *ridiculous*. Do we need that much for an emergency?"

"It's thirty-five pounds," reaffirmed Jim. "Not a pound less."

"What about a *sled*?"

"I've used them," Martyn said, somewhat perfunctorily.

I decided to get a sled on my own. This proved to be a more difficult task than I had anticipated.

I had used children's sleds on overnight cross-country ski trips before. They worked well, except that the holes used for the haul line and lashings tore out.

If I were to take a sled to the pole, I would have to solve that problem.

I finally found a good sled at the neighborhood gas station. It was a child's sled, made of hard, thick, and durable polyethylene, curved on all four sides, about 5 inches deep and large enough to hold a medium-sized backpack. It cost $9.95.

The only problem that I could determine was that the plastic holes would tear out from the strain of hauling.

Wondering whether the sleds would be suitable for an expedition such as ours, I called a manufacturer of expedition sleds in Colorado to ask his opinion.

"Are those the $10 children's sleds?" he asked.

"Yes."

"They will disintegrate long before you get to the pole," he assured me.

Just in case he was right, I added my $400 Smith expedition sled to the others, since by now we had decided on these sleds. I still intended to use the children's sleds and to recommend them to the others.

It seemed a little ludicrous—that a child's sled might do the job of a heavy expedition sled.

But my hunch was that the cheap sled might just make it all the way to the pole.

As September became October and October became November, the days shortened and so did the time to departure. My work schedule was such that whenever I turned to the problem of getting to the Antarctic, it was with a sense of relief and escape.

One morning I opened my mail to find the schedule to Santiago.

Nadia, Leo's wife, had booked me to Miami via

Detroit with a half-hour layover in Detroit. I called her and said the schedule was too tight. She advised me to check the bags to New York City and transfer them by myself. If the bags failed to arrive, I was told to have a copy of the Santiago ticket and to get it to the TWA baggage people, who would get them on a flight the next day.

A call came from Martyn asking whether everything was set. I said it was.

In turn, he told me that our expedition was down by one member: Reinette had called him to say that she was not going. She couldn't raise the money in time.

Friends invited Diana and me to a farewell dinner held the night before my departure.

Companions from other adventure trips came and presented Diana with an adorable stuffed penguin to take my place when I was gone. I was very touched by this show of support and affection.

The next morning was pure sadness. There were tears in Diana's eyes as we parted.

"I'll be safe," I tried to reassure her. "And I'll be back within two months. You'll see."

The ride to the airport to begin my great adventure was comic. The temperature was falling, it was snowing, and the streets were unplowed.

When my cab arrived late, I saw it was in a state of partial disintegration. The driver didn't know if he could make it.

"The trunk won't close," the cab driver lamented, "and I can't shut my door."

He didn't realize how well equipped I was to deal with the problem. I was, after all, headed to the South Pole.

"It's okay," I said, "I have my climbing rope."

To his amazement, I pulled the short nylon climbing rope out of my pack, and lashed his trunk shut. I attached another rope to the driver's door handle. I ducked my head around the skis, which ran from the front window to the back. Then, I held the door shut all the way to the airport as the driver peered through the misty front window, wipers flapping crazily at full speed.

But we had made it on time.

The Minneapolis-St. Paul International airport was nearly empty in the heavy snowfall. You couldn't see the planes on the runway, and the wide marble floor of the ticketing section was vacant.

I had five bags, which I had originally intended to check only to New York, following my travel agent's advice. But one bag was fitted with heat packs sent by Shirley, and I didn't particularly look forward to hauling them around.

"Check everything to Santiago?" The attendant insisted that it was perfectly safe. "That's the best way to do it; otherwise, we'll have to charge you extra twice."

I finally let her persuade me to send the skis and a second bag all the way to Santiago.

While I didn't care what happened to Shirley's heat packs, I did need the skis. I paid the $130 TWA surcharge, feeling as if I'd been both ripped off and misinformed.

I still had the fever that had plagued me for two days. I was hoping to shake it off before we got to the Antarctic, and I was glad I'd put on the wool underwear Shirley had sent everyone.

The wool would equalize my temperature and cut the work my body had to do to keep me warm. Nothing like long underwear to counteract disease, I thought.

Thankfully, the plane to New York was nearly empty, which gave me breathing space and comfort for my sickness. I worried about whether I had tipped the porter enough to ensure that he would take my skis downstairs for check-in, but then I saw the skis being loaded on the plane. The transfer in New York still remained a concern.

The more I travelled, the more I seemed to worry about whether my equipment would actually arrive in time. There would be only one flight from Chile to our base camp in the Antarctic, a 2,000-mile flight—the only flight.

If my equipment didn't reach Santiago, I couldn't replace it. It wasn't like losing a suit or a tie or a shoe. Santiago didn't have stores that sold Canadian military boots, size 11 wide, or three-pin-binding Telemark boots, or expedition sleeping bags good for -50 degrees Fahrenheit. In fact, only one store in Minneapolis carried such equipment, and not many cities in the United States had stores that did.

My equipment made it to New York anyway.

The weather in New York was clear, but the temperature had dropped sharply, the sky was overcast, and flocks of small birds were assembling in platoons for the flight south—perhaps by the same route I would take.

Since I was four hours early, I had time to check my bags at Lan Chile without waiting in line. The delay gave me a chance to have coffee and relax before the flight.

Jerry Corr arrived in New York a little later and he joined me on the Lan Chile flight to Miami. We had adjoining bulkhead seats which made the journey more pleasant. The blue-suited Lan Chile stewardesses served dinner, and Jerry and I chatted about the upcoming trip.

You would not suspect from looking at Jerry Corr how driven he was by a restless urge to high adventure. His blue eyes, graying beard, slight stature, and age gave little indication of that.

He had attempted the highest peak in South America,

tried a 26,000-foot-peak in the Himalayas, and was planning to go to Everest—all after the age of 50.

His work at home of running a family shopping-center management and development company was apparently no deterrence to Jerry's varied schemes for adventure.

After dinner, I fell asleep and slept right through the stop in Miami. Stuart and Lise were supposed to be there, but were not. They had missed the connection and planned to fly down the next day with all the skis.

We had met Lise briefly at our training in Whitehorse, where we were told she was to be the expedition physician and stationed at base camp during our entire trip. She planned to conduct medical research on our progress.

She, too, was a serious person.

Martyn told me the story of how she had been forced to leave her first trek in a remote part of the Yukon when her brand new boots turned out to be too small and caused massive blisters. Forced to fly out, she returned to the store where she got the boots, berated the owner for giving her the wrong size, secured a new pair, and, at her own considerable expense, chartered a plane back to finish the trek.

There was no question in my mind: Lise would be a tough and cheerful addition.

The airport was jammed with travelers, mainly Chilean, all trying to retrieve their baggage and get through customs. I could hear many conversations in Spanish, occasional German, and a smattering of English from the two Mountain Travel groups there, ours and another destined for hiking in the south.

Our baggage came last, the large red duffels we each had, our personal bags, and miscellaneous other gear.

I searched for my red ski bag, but in vain. It was missing.

A helpful Lan Chile representative took the baggage numbers and promised to wire New York.

I was disappointed about the lost bag, but there was nothing I could do. For the six of us—Ron, Tori, Jerry, J. K., Jim, and me—there were 27 bags. I alone had four.

We stayed overnight in Santiago, and the next day, we were back at the airport again, heading ever south. The airport lobby was filled with tourists, mostly Chilean, men, women, and children plus a few foreigners.

Ever one to save money, Jim insisted on getting the team's precious 27 bags on the plane at no surcharge.

"We were 500 kilos overweight," he confessed.

"I don't think you can get all that in without paying more," I said.

But he did—or so we thought.

As we headed out for the plane, we watched in surprise as our bags were unloaded from the plane and returned to the airport.

"Serves us right," I said. But Jim was unperturbed.

"The plane is probably overloaded," he countered.

The plane was completely full. I found myself seated on the aisle next to two gray-habited nuns. Neither spoke English, but they offered me the window seat when they discovered I wanted to take pictures. They were about my age, one strikingly handsome with gray hair and brown eyes and dressed in a light gray habit.

"Expedicion al Polo Sur?" one asked.

"Si."

She looked up worriedly. "That's a dangerous undertaking. Are you sure it's wise?" But then she caught herself and merely added, "Buenos expediciones."

We landed in a high wind, the plane buffeting in the rough weather of Punta Arenas, the town that borders the treacherous Strait of Magellan. As we boarded the bus that would take us to town, I looked at the bleak landscape.

We were in the land that bordered the feared Tierra del Fuego, where winds reached 110 knots and many a ship had been dashed to pieces on the rocks while attempting to make it through the treacherous passage.

What would it be like flying across that strait? I wondered. The trees along the road were short and stunted from the wind. The land seemed bleak, barren, and hard.

It made me realize we were at the end of the continent, near the very end of the earth.

We entered Punta Arenas by the main street, circled Magellan Square, with its large statue of the explorer, and stopped at a small hotel on one corner.

Jerry and I were quartered in a small room on the third floor, with Ron and J. K. down the hall in a double, and Jim and Tori each with separate rooms.

There was no sign of Shirley, who, we were told, had a room in the fancy hotel across the square.

Jerry and I didn't have much space, since our bags filled the small room. The hotel, which had once been a residence hotel, was being refurbished as a commercial hotel. A new bathroom with a modern toilet was off in one corner. From the curtained single window, I could just see the town square in the distance.

Eventually, our baggage caught up with us. I parked my red bag and two duffels in the corner to give more space. Then I began the task of deciding what to leave here in Punta Arenas and what to take with me.

At last, I met Alejo Contreras-Steading, the Chilean representative who would be going with us to the South Pole. Alejo was about 30, slim, and tall, with black hair but the beginnings of a red beard. He had a boyish look.

"My English teacher said many years ago," he shyly

admitted, "that I should concentrate on my pronunciation, but I didn't. I never thought I'd need English."

Martyn told me later, "He doesn't own a suit coat but had to borrow one to meet Chilean officials. Half the time he puts on his Patagonia jacket inside out."

This was quite observant of Martyn, who seemed to have no concern whatsoever about his own attire.

To carry our food, tents, personal clothing, sleeping bags, and gasoline, we would depend on two specially constructed, large expedition sledges, similar to sledges made in Alaska.

Each sledge was roughly 20 feet long by 4 feet wide and 8 inches high. Each would be towed by a snowmobile.

When empty, the sledges weighed over 100 pounds each. Loaded, the two could carry over a ton of food and equipment. When fully loaded, its height would come up to my chest.

Built in Punta Arenas to Martyn's specifications, the sledges were meant to trail behind the snowmobiles over the rough sastrugi, where the force of the hard ice-like snow was enough to shear steel bolts and twist steel blades.

Consequently, the sledges had to be made out of something better than iron or steel. It had to be constructed of materials that *could give*, when subjected to force—resilient materials that could rebound.

The solution was to have *wooden* runners that would be attached to wooden crossbars by thin *nylon strings*.

Under pressure, the nylon would stretch and the wooden blades would bend so that the sledges could travel over the hard Antarctic surface without breaking.

That was the theory, at least.

Martyn was pleased. "The sledges are being finished," he announced. "We'll leave tomorrow on schedule."

Final decisions had to be made on equipment, and so we met after breakfast. Everyone was there, including Shirley.

We also now met Mike Sharp, the wild-haired English snowmobile driver whom I met for the first time.

He was tall, over six feet, with a wild shock of brown hair, and a wonderful sense of irony. He had gone to college with Martyn, though he was two years younger, and had majored in mathematics.

He had spent seven years in the Antarctic with the British Antarctic Survey, part of it running the British station at Rothera. Mike was the most articulate member of our group and, I suspect, the smartest. He had wanted to go on Steger's Greenland and Transantarctic expeditions when Martyn dropped out as the English member, but someone else was chosen.

Each time Martyn asked him to join our South Pole Overland Expedition, he simply laughed. But in the end, he came. And I was glad he was with us.

We later found out that Shirley had come to Chile a *week* before the rest of us and also had arrived at Punta Arenas ahead of the team..

"This hotel was full," she had tried to explain to us, "so I had to stay across the square."

We suspected she looked at the accommodations and simply fled to a more expensive hotel.

The final meeting was somewhat raucous. Martyn, Stuart, and Mike had just come in from a morning cocktail party and were in little mood for the long series of serious questions that would be put to them by J. K. and Shirley.

After Mike pretended to pump up Martyn like a balloon so he could talk, Martyn did manage to give a coherent plan of our intended operations:

We would start at Patriot Hills; fly to Hercules Inlet from 80 degrees west, 80 degrees south, and then ski the 30 miles back to Patriot Hills, before continuing on to the pole. Supplies for our journey south would arrive by two airdrops at predesignated locations.

I watched them roll out the enormous map that covered much of the floor of the hotel dining room and observed Martyn tracing our route.

"Snowmobiles will follow," Martyn remarked.

At that, J. K. perked up his head. He now had a lot of questions: "What is the snowmobile plan? How far will the snowmobiles be at the maximum from the skiers? What is the standard operating procedure?"

On hearing the questions, Martyn turned to Mike, who deliberately intoned in jest. *"Plan? What do you mean plan?"*

"Your standard operating procedure. And how you will prevent loss in a crevasse?" pursued J. K.

"Crevasse?" jested Mike. "What do you mean *crevasse?"*

At that, Tori interrupted the low comedy to explain to J.K. in detail the rescue plan for the snowmobiles. She remembered it perfectly from our instruction in the Alaska training session.,

"That's it," said Mike. "They will all be tied together like climbers on a rope."

He looked at Martyn: "Is that all right, Martyn? Is that a *good* answer?"

The comedy of the situation did not quite amuse J. K., who was in dead earnest, or Shirley, who was clearly containing her emotions at the somewhat drunken duo. Ron and Jerry were completely silent.

"When I talked with Hillary in London," J. K. continued, referring to the famous New Zealand climber, Edmund Hillary, "I spent an *hour* with him. He stressed over and over that the snowmobiles be no more than 1,000 meters from the skiers. The skiers should be roped up, for the crevasses are very dangerous."

He paused and then added, "I'm only quoting what Hillary said."

I looked for a sign on Martyn's face but could detect

none. Obviously, his expertise and authority were being questioned. At the very least, his plan was being queried.

J. K. had had a lot of snowmobile experience in the Antarctic when he had headed the Indian station. He had lost in the effort to pinpoint our exact route on the 1:50,000 maps he earlier insisted existed somewhere in the United States. Earlier in this meeting, Martyn had showed us what maps he had and what he did not have. The larger-scale maps were available only for the first part of the journey, not the latter.

Martyn started to explain again that the snowmobiles would go second. It would be a much more pleasant trip for us that way, he reasoned. It would seem more as if we were unsupported and on our own. "We will play it by ear," he said. "We'll see what works best."

J. K. reiterated the 1,000-meter rule and then persisted, "What if one snowmobile goes down a crevasse and the skiers are 20 kilometers away? What then?"

"The skiers will have survival equipment. They can last for 24 hours," Martyn replied.

"But in the Antarctic?" asked J. K. "You can have 10-day storms."

At that, Martyn explained how the four of them—he, Mike, Stuart, and Jim—had many years of experience.

He also added, "We have tested the sledges."

It was the very sledge design that J. K. had criticized as being too heavy and too long as well as being inferior to the sledges made in Germany.

"We tested it here and in Canada," Martyn replied resolutely. "It *will work*."

That seemed to settle the questions from J. K.

Now it was Shirley's turn. Not to be outdone, she pulled out a list of questions. Running one hand through her blond hair, she began: "I have some personal questions. First, what do we *wear*?"

Martyn could not resist.

"I'm wearing *pink*," he replied. "The plane will be red and black. So pink seems most appropriate."

He got a laugh as Shirley grimaced slightly.

Then Martyn patiently explained: "We should dress lightly. Wear pile pants and jackets and windbreakers to take off in the airplane, which will be hot. Don't put too much in your pack."

I realized that the procedure and clothing requirements had been stated before, but Shirley had been off somewhere and had not heard. Even so, I was glad to hear the instructions repeated, because Martyn talked very fast.

Next, Shirley asked about the gear that would be "taken out" to base camp for the skiers and about gear brought in from base camp when the plane made its resupply runs.

"Taken out?" asked Martyn. "What do you mean?"

"Well, spare batteries, change of underwear," said Shirley.

"How much underwear did you bring?" I queried.

"Well, you know, spare Kotex."

Martyn frowned.

"I think if you need something you'd better bring it with you. And only the bare essentials."

On my own, I had purchased and brought to Punta Arenas nine children's plastic sleds—one for each of us. This was so that we wouldn't have to carry our emergency gear in packs if we didn't want to.

From experience, I knew that it was much easier to haul a sled behind skis than to carry a heavy pack.

Though the sleds were simple, cheap things, I'd rigged them carefully with hauling lines and ties so that they would be easy to manage and would hold the emergency gear securely inside.

I had only two concerns: Would Martyn agree to take

the sleds? And would these $10 children's sleds make it to the South Pole without disintegrating?

I had no way of knowing the answer to either question. I felt it was time to get an answer to the first question.

"Do you want to see the sleds?" I asked hesitatingly.

Martyn looked as if that was the last thing he wanted to see.

"Later," he said. *"Perhaps* later."

"I have one ready. I'll bring it in," I offered.

I went to my room to get one of the sleds and the pack I had already rigged inside it.

Returning to the assembly, I demonstrated how the sled was to be pulled, how everything was reinforced, and how to use the knots.

"The bottom's very smooth," Martyn said. To my surprise, he seemed pleased.

It was agreed. We would take the sleds with us to Antarctica.

That decided, only the second questioned remained: Would the little sleds actually survive the long journey to the pole?

Just as the sun faded away, we followed Martyn out into the darkened streets of town. Even the Catholic church on the square was locked, its front gate shut.

It was time for our last supper—the last meal we'd have in civilization for some time.

We walked down one side street toward a fancy restaurant a block from the wharf, but it was filled, and we moved on to Martyn's favorite eating place, where the meat was cooked on an enormous broiler. The rest of the team was already there, ensconced at a nearby table.

It was past 10:00 p.m. when we arrived, and by the time we finished stuffing ourselves, it was well past midnight.

The wind was light as we strode back to the hotel; clouds covered the sky. I was glad to turn in, though some of the others didn't return till the early hours of the morning.

I stripped off my city clothes, put on my wool underwear for pajamas, and crawled underneath the heavy blanket.

I dreamed of ice and snow and of the pole that lay ahead, visions forming in my mind of the long journey.

And once again, I woke up in a sweat—wondering whether I could make it.

5 / FLIGHT TO
BASE CAMP

JIM WAS IN THE DOORWAY. "We'll leave
tomorrow morning. Have your bags in the entrance at
6:00 a.m.," he announced, cautioning us: "Take only
your red bag, *no more*."

Cutting down to one red bag was not easy for any of
us. Shirley, with all her video equipment, had particular
difficulty. Martyn already had asked Shirley to
eliminate some of her baggage, and then Stuart had told
her emphatically, "You can't take those *three* bags.
They're too much!"

Jim sent Tori off to repeat the message. "Tell Shirley
we're going to weigh the bags in an hour and tell her to
get it all in *one* bag." Then as an aside, he told her,
"We're actually not weighing them right away, but
Shirley won't be done unless she thinks that."

I could visualize the forthcoming scene. Shirley

probably had an outfit for each day, plus three dozen batteries for her VCR camera. Yet she would have to pick and choose, and leave some behind, just like the rest of us.

We already had more stuff than we could use. Jim's room was filled with the chemically powered warmers Shirley had sent each of us. Martyn had said that they didn't work very well and we shouldn't take them.

On the matter of deciding what to keep and what to leave behind, I had to sympathize somewhat with Shirley. I planned to wear my ski suit, heavy parka and Canadian military boots.

Although I managed to get the rest of my gear into the red bag, it was only with great difficulty. In the bag, I put two pairs of Telemark boots, the Merrills, Berghaus gaiters, one pair of Solomon boots, three pairs of polypropylene underwear (one heavy, one medium, and one light), pile pants and jacket, down pants, two pairs of shell pants, one shell jacket, and two sets of bib pants.

I also had to get in two sets of goggles with mask, four pairs of mitts, a radio, one jumar, five carabiners, a down sleeping bag, a bivouac sack, two sleeping-bag liners, five pairs of socks and a 40-foot length of climbing rope.

In addition, I needed my small camera, my VBL socks. Plus other odds and ends.

It was too much. I had far more than I needed.

But I was not sure what to keep and what to discard.

What I would ultimately need depended on the wind and temperature in the Antarctic and how difficult it would be to regulate my body temperature.

I rationalized the excess. I was taking two pairs of Telemark boots because I wanted to use the light pair, if possible, not the heavy pair. Only by taking both would I have a choice.

Martyn thought the heavy Berghaus gaiters and the heavy boots were essential. But I couldn't get the gaiters over the boots; the rubber of the bottom of the gaiter was extremely tight and had to be stretched to the limit to fit over the boot. Only Jim was able to get the gaiters on, and perspiration beaded on his forehead as he struggled to do so.

Shirley, at the latest report, had eliminated one of her three bags.

The next morning dawned clear and bright. The duffels had to be brought to the airport early to be weighed in for the flight.

I was cautious about my back, which I had broken climbing years ago. I knew I'd have to be careful, or I'd be out of commission quickly. I slid my red duffel down two flights of stairs to the entrance, rather than carrying it. Then, because Jerry's back was hurting, I slid his bag down.

The next event in the morning was an interview with the local radio station in Punta Arenas. We were all seated by the fireplace in front of the hotel desk, while a young woman with a Nikon camera snuck pictures of each of us when she thought we weren't looking. The reporter asked questions in Spanish, which the hotel receptionist translated into English.

I was the last to be interviewed. The questions came in rapid succession: "Are you too old to do the trip? What does your wife think about this expedition?"

I answered that although I was 58, I did not consider myself too old to do the trip, and that my wife was reluctant to have me go and worried.

"How did you train?"

"With the best of intentions—one week into training I broke my collar bone. That ended my good intentions."

The reporter laughed and asked no more questions of me.

The photographer asked us to go down to the street and assemble in the town square for a photograph in front of Magellan's statue.

As we posed for the shots, we were caught in the crossfire of a water-bomb war between two groups of uniformed high school boys who raced back and forth under the shrubbery and trees of the square.

Doused, we had no chance to dry out, for when we got back to the hotel, the taxi was waiting. Tori, Ron, Jerry, and I got in. Shirley was not yet to be seen, and J. K. was still upstairs in the hotel.

We waited for the taxi driver to start for the airport, but he did nothing. We simply sat and waited, not knowing what would happen next.

Suddenly, it occurred to me that the taxi driver had no idea of where we wished to go.

"Aero Puerto," I shouted, *"Aero Puerto,"* recalling the only word in Spanish I knew for our destination. Off we went.

White clouds covered the horizon in the distance, and the wind swept across the stunted grass and trees. Flags were stretched straight out, and branches of trees were bent sharply downward by the force of the wind. The houses we passed looked peeled and worn from the constant beating of the wind

Martyn, Stuart, and Alejo had already arrived at the airport to weigh in our baggage. Each of us stepped onto the airport scale, while Martyn recorded the figure. He needed our weight for calibrating the load on the DC-4 and for Lise, who wished to estimate our loss of body fat and weight during the trip. When I got on the scale, it showed 106 kilograms, but I had no idea what that meant in pounds.

After the customs officials gave up their demand to check our luggage, we descended the stairs and hiked out to the planes, forming a long, straggling line in the sunlight. I watched the members of our expedition and the climbers destined for Mount Vinson in climbing outfits and packs as they crossed the runway.

The orange and silver colors of the DC-4 glistened in the distance, but as I reached the plane, I could see that the bright image was deceptive. The plane was a World War II craft, half a century old, and the worn metal looked its age. A year ago, mechanical problems had delayed departures and prevented some climbing parties from reaching the Antarctic.

Yet we had to rely upon this ancient airplane to fly us nearly 2,000 miles, including 500 miles over the treacherous Drake Passage, where winds could reach over 110 knots.

That could be a little tricky, considering that the flying speed of the DC-4 was just 170 knots and it could carry just enough fuel for the flight. That also meant we could not make our destination against high winds.

I climbed the steel stairway to the aircraft, and had to blink a few times as I stepped inside. In the dim light, I saw a miniature mountain of gear, duffel bags, packs, and skis all lashed down by large straps on the left side of the plane. Beyond the gear gleamed large metal tanks of extra fuel; in the rear of the plane were the utilitarian seats, set in rows of two against aluminum exterior walls. This was clearly not a typical comfortable passenger plane.

I selected a seat near the window, jammed my pack under the seat ahead of me, and buckled myself in. There was no heat: I could almost see my breath. I kept my heavy parka, pile hat, and mittens on.

Within a few minutes, we were ready for takeoff. There were 27 seats and 27 bodies, including the 11 members of the South Pole Overland Expedition.

The captain of the plane was Colin Campbell, a heavy man, clad in a one-piece down suit streaked with grease. He told us not to move about or the pilot would continuously have to adjust the trim of the aircraft. Within a few hours we would violate that advice, but for the moment, everyone sat tight, buckled in.

"Life vests are under your seats," Colin continued. "It will be a 10-hour flight. Make yourselves comfortable," he added, as if that were possible.

The engines sputtered as the pilot warmed up the plane and ran through the checklist. When we turned into the wind for takeoff, I took one last look at civilization and reminded myself that I would not see it again for another two months.

The dull green of the fields below near Punta Arenas quickly gave way to water and then clouds as the DC-4 turned south.

Slowly, we rose until we reached an altitude of 8,000 feet.

Every hour, Martyn circulated a sheet that gave our altitude, airspeed, latitude, and longitude. Each hour, I watched the latitude rise from 50 degrees south at Punta Arenas to successively higher numbers.

We were heading for Patriot Hills, which was nearly 80 degrees south and 1,900 miles south of Punta Arenas, and 690 miles north of the South Pole.

For the first half hour, clouds obscured the view. But then they dropped below, in a blanket of white, until we came to the open sea.

Over most of this distance, what I saw mostly was a large white blank at the bottom of the earth the size of the continental U.S. and Mexico combined.

As we came in over the sea, I caught my first glimpse of Antarctica. There it was, lying below me.

For months, I had dreamed of this remote land of ice and snow, but nothing I had read, little of the pictures I had seen, had given me much impression of the real thing.

I saw a blank sheet of white stretching across a sea of dark blue. Its edge was not straight but slightly irregular, a randomly drawn edge jutting up from the ocean.

"Shelf ice," someone had said. As I looked more carefully, I could see what seemed to be cracks in the ice. I had no idea how thick the ice was or how long it had been there.

We flew over the ice sheet for what seemed more than an hour and then, fairly quickly, the ice's flatness gave way to low-lying hills and then low mountains. The peaks were snow-covered, quite beautiful, with long ranges angling south.

"The Ellsworth Mountains," someone said.

The Ellsworth range ran in long ridges with wide valleys and couloirs separating one peak from the next. I could see that the mountains were not ancient, for their features were too sharp for that. From this height, I had the distinct impression they seemed gentle, especially with the blanket of snow that soothed the range. But the peaks, I knew, were all nearly virgin and unclimbed.

It was a strange world, a sea of white extending for thousands of miles, punctuated by isolated peaks and occasional ranges that thrust up through the glistening snow.

From this height, I could only imagine what it would be like.

Not once did I see the crevasses that I had worried about—the cracks in the enormous shield of ice that might be ready to devour us or trap our machines if we were not wary enough to spot them or not cautious enough to use a safety line.

My thoughts on the landscape below were interrupted by a call for lunch. We helped ourselves to slices of cheese and ham, inserted between bread or heavy crackers, and to white and brown chocolate bars as well as to cans of yogurt.

After a time, we became unconscious of the deadly drone of the engines and the shudder of the metal floor of the cabin. We soon began to roam about the cabin, forgetting the earlier warning to stay buckled in. Ahead, I saw Mike sprawled out on the duffel and Shirley stretched across two seats.

Just as I was dozing off, I found Stuart in the seat next to me. "I want to conduct a survey," he said.

"On what?" I asked.

"On your feelings about the trip and the group. I wish to take the survey now and then compare it with another one later in the trip."

I was getting a little bored with all the questions. I had already filled out Lise's psychological test, the California Multiphasic, which asked whether I was disturbed by hearing voices, feelings of anger, or inability to concentrate or get things done.

Now Stuart was asking more. Why was I going? How did I think the group would get along? Were they prepared for such a trip?

I tried to get through them as quickly as possible. I said I was on board for the adventure of the trip, and nothing more; I repeated that prior expedition experience was important, but on later reflection, I wasn't sure it was. I remembered that the most experienced were sometimes the most difficult and the least adaptive. On this expedition, everyone had extensive expedition experience, except Ron and Shirley.

I was glad to be spared some of the last questions when Colin announced that we would be descending in a few minutes.

A mile or two distant a large ridge appeared. It was black and layered, a sedimentary rock, I guessed, not granite. The flank below the wing of the plane was not snow-covered like the peaks beyond. I had never seen a ridge quite like it, though it certainly was not atypical of mountain topography. A low ramp of snow rose just beyond, separating the black ridge from the white ridge in the distance.

Below the ridge, I saw an odd, sparkling plain.

For a moment, I thought it was water. Though it appeared like a flat sea wafted by a light breeze, it was not water, but blue ice pocketed by sun cups—small pockmarks in the surface made by the sun.

In the low light, the blue ice was dark, but later when I could observe it more closely, I saw that the color was pale blue, a blue reminiscent of glacial lakes. The surface was deceptively calm, but held a treachery for anyone who thought to cross it by ski. I knew the skis would slip easily, and a fall on the hard surface would come as a sudden jolt, enough to knock you senseless.

Beyond the sparkling blue ice of the air field, great glaciers spilled down from the granite peaks above, their surfaces bathed in white.

The scene was magnificent in the eternal light of the Antarctic summer. Though the sun was low in the sky and circling south, it did not drop from sight and would not for several months.

We were now in the land of continuous daylight. I was curious about the effect of constant sunlight, which I had never experienced before.

The pilot made a full 360-degree approach and lowered the flaps into the wind. I watched the brown flanks of the hills rise above me and saw the pockmarked plain of blue ice.

I heard the wheels hit the surface and then watched the ice race beneath.

The plane bounced and swerved and then came to a stop with a jerk.

We were here!

The aircraft door flew open with a bang and frigid air rushed in. I grappled to get my warm parka and mittens on, items I'd thrown off when the plane heated up. I pulled my goggles out of my pack, unbuckled my seat belt, and edged toward the door.

I felt the cold as I first stepped out of the open door of the DC4. The sudden chill was like walking into a deep freeze from a warm room.

The deep cold seemed to move through my many layers of down and to penetrate my skin.

I yanked up my zipper and pulled the cords of my hood tighter; then I tightened the drawstring on my mitts.

But the cold persisted—it was not to be stopped.

It was a deep, penetrating cold that gradually reached beneath my skin right to my inner core.

Momentary panic hit me: *Would I ever be warm again?*

The shock of the cold was enough to warn me not to remove my gloves and not to touch the aluminum sides of the ladder that led from the warm belly of the plane to the ice below.

If I touched the icy metal, the skin of my bare hands would stick to the metal and tear off. That, I knew from painful childhood experience, was one certain danger of the Antarctic.

I glanced up at the sun and then looked away, for it was full and bright. The strong, yellow beam could damage my eyes if I stared directly at it.

I fumbled for my pocket, took off my right-hand mitt, unzipped the cold metal zipper, drew out my dark green glacial goggles. I lifted them up and somewhat awkwardly pulled them over my pile hat, trying not to lose the hat as I did so.

As I moved from the plane, I felt a blast of air.

It was the *Antarctic wind*, a wind I had heard about, read about, even dreamed about. I had wondered how strong this wind would be, what it would do to our progress, and whether we could ski against it.

I had not figured its effects on our bodies or the added cold it would inflict.

It was stupid of me not to have known. The wind-chill factor had been developed in Antarctica as a means of knowing how much insulation man needed to withstand the cold.

I had thought about the cold, but had completely forgotten the wind—a wind that could turn 20 degrees above Fahrenheit into 20 degrees below in a matter of seconds and alter near-comfort to danger of death if protection was not soon at hand.

I had not counted on the wind, had not remembered enough to fear it, not even considered its potentially deadly impact upon my body and health. Now I knew the wind was here and felt it.

I tried to guess the wind speed. Years of wind surfing, where each day I had to estimate the speed of the air to select the proper size sail, had made me somewhat knowledgeable. I judged the speed to be 18 knots, which was roughly one-sixth less than the speed in miles per hour. Thirty plus one-sixth of 18 made 21 miles per hour.

Perhaps it was the wind that made the chill. Then, I reasoned it was just the cold, the notorious Antarctica cold that Scott had described so emotionally and that had stopped so many men in their futile attempts to reach the South Pole.

Would we, too, be felled by the painful cold? I doubted it at first, but as the intensity of the cold continued, I began to doubt even my own certainty. I began to wonder.

The plane crew understandably was eager to get the craft unloaded in the sharp wind. As they handed the cargo out of the fuselage, we carried it away and stacked it.

The work of unloading began to make me forget the cold, and the energy I used warmed my blood. I forgot where I was. My body seemed to warm. But the warmth was not to last. When the work stopped, the heat ceased. I shivered once again.

Martyn had brought one of the sledges from the Patriot Hills camp, a quarter of a mile away, and we soon had it loaded. Martyn headed toward camp in the wind and drifting snow.

Halfway to camp, one of the wooden blades of the sledge twisted underneath and the crippled sledge lurched to a stop, unable to move.

It had broken down after 200 yards.

And we were counting on it to make it to the South Pole!

The accident did not bode well for our success. The second sledge was brought, and, fortunately, it held up for the short haul from the DC-4 to camp.

I rode the top of the load, bracing myself so I wouldn't be thrown to the ground or trampled underneath if the sledge tipped over. The load banked this way and that on the hard waves of snow.

The Patriot Hills camp was set up on a flat field of snow on the surface of the level ice. It consisted of a row of four canvas Quonset hut-like structures, each the shape of a half cylinder roughly 40 feet long, 20 feet wide, and 10 feet tall. The walls of the tents were insulated and held up by aluminum struts.

One tent served as a supply room, two as bedrooms,

and the last and largest, as a combination kitchen, dining room, and recreation area.

The Twin Otter was parked to the side of the last tent. We unloaded our equipment and stacked it up in piles near camp.

To the west of camp lay the Patriot Hills. To the east, the land was flat and unmarked by anything except two distant nunataks and another camp consisting of two canvas Quonsets and two Twin Otters. This belonged to the Chilean Air Force, I learned, and they would be here only 15 days.

In the cook tent, I saw Lise and met Henry Perk, the Twin Otter pilot, and Gordon Wiltsie, the *National Geographic* photographer. Henry, a tall, heavy man, was Swiss, from St. Moritz, and a former Canadian Mountain Holiday ski guide. He had been flying in the Antarctic for many years now. I suspected that it was partly because of Henry that Lise had come back to the Antarctic.

Gordon was on assignment to take pictures of us and was the leader of a forthcoming two-week ski tour. Tall, trim, and articulate, he had been to the Antarctic before.

It was late in the day, and I was glad to head off to my sleeping bag. Martyn had assigned us to tents: Jerry and I to one, the two colonels to a second, and the two women to a third.

The choice of Jerry for a tentmate was good, for he was considerate, a businessman, a mountain climber about the same age as I, and Irish. We had much in common.

After helping Jerry put up the tent, I announced I would sleep outside in my bivouac sack.

Wishing him a good night's rest, I stepped outside to the Antarctic night and began to assemble my sleeping gear.

I pulled out my yellow Gortex outer bag, stuffed a

Chouinard Thinsulite bag inside my down Marmot bag, and lined up the bag with the head to the south and my duffel just beyond it as a barrier against the wind.

I often slept in my bivouac sack outside under the stars, and I preferred it to the confines of the tent, even in winter.

Here it had been merely a matter of slipping off my one-piece suit and crawling into the bag. Since there was no wind, that was not difficult or uncomfortable. The fit was a little snug, but after my body heated up the bag, I was warm. I carefully placed my pee bottle within reach so I wouldn't have to crawl out into the cold in the middle of the night.

After slipping my eye mask over my eyes for protection against the light, I gradually drifted off to sleep. Tomorrow, I reflected, we will work on the broken sledge and prepare food packs. It will be a day of preparation for the journey that would begin two days from now.

Again, momentary doubts crossed my mind. Was I too old, too overweight, or too out of shape?

Then I started to reassure myself.

If I can manage the first week, I can do the second week. If I can get through the second week, I think I can do the rest of it.

The key would be to get through the first week. That thought was comforting.

Compared to the others, I was not as strong. Jim had just returned from three weeks of hiking in Bhutan, Martyn was in superb condition, Shirley had been training like a professional athlete all summer, and Jerry ran up and down three flights of stairs with a pack on his back every day. Tori performed a heavy schedule of exercise, and Ron, a triathloner, trained every day on a cross-country machine. I didn't know much about J. K., who was a colonel in the Indian army, but he certainly looked in shape.

My sole advantage was my past skiing and expedition experience. Only Jerry, Jim, and I had been on long expeditions at high altitude. Yet long-distance cross-country skiing might be entirely different from mountaineering expeditions. As I fell asleep this first night in the snow, I realized that the next days would tell me whether I could make it.

It was not the sun that awoke me the next morning, for the sun had been up all night. Perhaps it was the cold.

After I crawled out of my bag, I pulled my red suit out of the Dana duffel and struggled into it. The suit was warm because hot air from my legs and body did not escape at the waist but remained trapped. It was like being in a cocoon.

Martyn was already up and bustling about. "The sledges must be repaired and the food packed," he announced, asking for volunteers.

I chose to work on the sledges, as did Tori and J. K. Ron and Jerry chose to pack the food. Shirley chose to take videos of our efforts.

We had brought 50 days of food for the expedition; part had been purchased in Canada, the rest, in Chile. The food was packaged as it had come from the store, but not in the daily food allotments we needed.

Unfortunately, the plastic bags needed to carry each day's allotment had not all arrived in Patriot Hills, so we had to improvise using the food cartons.

There were 17 different menus. The bag for each day was numbered by the day it was to be used. Some things, like sugar and cocoa and coffee, were left in the original cans, which were then marked by the number of days they were to be used—one, two, or three days.

The food was standard expedition food, not freeze-dried but whole food: beef, lamb, carrots, potatoes, spaghetti, curry, and stew for dinner; and oatmeal, granola, and pancakes for breakfast. For lunch, we would have dried fruit, peanut butter and jelly, bread, and crackers.

Laying out the bags and dividing the food took most of the day. When I was not working on the sledge, I helped to prepare 20 days of food to take with us. We stored the rest in a large snow pit under canvas for later retrieval. It was essential to dig a pit, or the drums of fuel and other supplies left outside would be scattered by the 60-knot storms.

The broken sledge had to be repaired quickly, for we planned to start the next day.

Its general structure resembled an old-fashioned child's sled: two long runners attached to a flat surface. The runners were 2-by-8-inch boards, each 20 feet long, with Teflon strips attached to the bottom. The top of the sledge was a series of 1-by-3-inch boards laid at right angles atop the blades. No metal was used, except for screws that attached the Teflon runners to the bottom of the blades.

The slats, set one-half-inch apart, were attached to the blade by slender nylon threads about one-sixteenth-inch thick. The threads had been incorrectly tied and had to be removed, restrung, and retied.

Since J. K. was skeptical of the sledge design, he insisted on making a second nylon wrapping. He and Tori did most of the work, though the rest of us pitched in.

Mike and Stuart prepared the Ski-Doos and filled small, red plastic fuel containers with the proper mixture of gasoline and oil. Shirley was off most of the day with her VCR camera, taking shots of our work, the camp, and the scenery.

By the end of the day, we were nearly ready for our expedition.

Our camp at Patriot Hills was 30 miles north of the

land edge of the continent, on Hercules Inlet, bordering the Ronne Ice Shelf.

We planned to send the Ski-Doos with the loaded sledges down the following morning to the very edge of the Ronne Ice Shelf. Later that day, we nine skiers planned to fly in the Twin Otter to the same spot. It was the Ronne Ice Shelf's edge that would be the official starting point of the expedition.

Over the following three days, we would ski past Patriot Hills again on our route to the pole.

In the evening, we assembled in the mess tent for dinner. I watched the hot lasagna being spooned out, a welcome offering after the long day of work on the sledge and food.

Dinner was a happy affair. At last, we were about to commence the expedition that we had looked forward to for so long.

The day broke clear, with bright sun and no clouds.

After breakfast, Mike and Stuart completed the final lashings on the sledges, loaded them with our gear, and set off in the Ski-Doos to head for our official starting point.

Later, when the radio call came that the Ski-Doos were in position, we hauled our packs over to the plane and loaded it with skis and sleeping bags. I climbed aboard and took a seat just behind Lise, who was flying down for the ride. Martyn occupied the co-pilot's seat to help direct the flight, and Gordon Wiltsie joined us with the intent of skiing back to Patriot Hills with us so he could take photographs.

We flew at an altitude of 1,000 feet, heading almost directly north. To our left lay the Ellsworth Mountains; to our right, a flat plain of snow extending unbroken to the horizon. Halfway to our destination, we passed a nunatak, a low hill that penetrated the ice and snow just to the left of our route.

When Henry spotted the Ski-Doos below, he circled, then lined the aircraft up with the markings Stuart and Mike had put down, reduced his speed, and headed in on the makeshift airfield. We hit the snow with a thud and then skidded and bounced to a stop.

We had arrived at the starting point.

I unbuckled my seat belt and followed the others out of the cabin door at the rear of the plane. As I looked down, I could see the flat white surface below, and when I reached the ground, I felt a gust of wind from the south.

Henry began passing out skis, packs, and tents. Once the plane was unloaded, we lined up for a picture, the whole group, arm in arm. Gordon took two pictures with each of our cameras.

It was an exciting moment.

In a few minutes, the airplane would depart.

I hugged Lise and said goodbye to Henry. Then we watched the plane rise slowly into the wind, circle once in a wide sweep, and then head north for Patriot Hills. We waved as the plane passed over, and we took pictures of its departure.

We were alone on the ice.

Though it was growing late, much remained to be done before we could turn in. The first task was to erect the mess tent. The giant tent lay on the sledge, folded up where it looked like an enormous rug.

To put up the tent, we folded it out twice, first lengthwise and then width-wise, and then stretched it out flat. Next, Jerry and Martyn crawled inside to push up the semicircular hinged aluminum struts that held the roof up. After we extended the base struts and added three more roof interior struts, the tent was erect, a great, yellow, oblong dome that looked like an enormous loaf of bread.

To keep frost and water from dripping inside the tent,

we added the white frost liner, attaching the Velcro straps to the inside struts of the tent. To nail the beast down, we staked its guy lines down on the ice.

When the mess tent was up, we carried in plastic food boxes, covered them with sheets of plywood for kitchen and dining tables, and added stools and the radio. The radio would enable us to communicate with Patriot Hills and Punta Arenas.

We lined the two-man sleeping tents up with the mess tent, three on each side, each pointed into the wind. Jerry placed our tent quite far out, "in the suburbs," as he put it, so we would not be disturbed by the noise in the mess tent. Jerry and I were on the east, next to the two colonels, who were beside Jim and Alejo. The mess tent was in the center, then the two women, next Martyn and Stuart, and, finally, Mike, alone.

The fare for each day was packed in a large plastic bag containing roughly two cubic feet of food. Within the walls of the bag were enough breakfasts, lunches, and dinners for eleven people.

At the south end of the tent was laid a long plywood board, set on three large plastic containers that held pots, pans, and other supplies. Martyn had pulled out the three MSR stoves, three pots, and a large spoon and ladle.

It was time to begin dinner. Martyn took one MSR and unscrewed the cap of an aluminum pint bottle of white gas. He inserted the stove fuel line inside the top of the fuel bottle and screwed it in tight.

He was careful to hold the bottle upright so no gas would spill out or touch his hands. Spilled white gas at this temperature would freeze his hands immediately. Then he gently opened the fuel gas valve part way and allowed fuel to seep into the holding pan of the stove.

Next Martyn pulled out a cigarette lighter from his pocket and lit the gas in the stove pan and allowed it to burn slowly. A yellow flame appeared and the stove began to heat. As it did, he began to pump the stove to build up pressure inside the fuel tank. The flame shot up four feet, nearly singeing the fabric fly on the ceiling of the tent.

I jumped up, but before I reached the cook table, Martyn had turned down the valve. The flame dropped to a few inches, and soon turned blue. As it did, the pressure built up in the stove and the gas coming out began to vaporize. Soon the flame was a deep blue, all trace of yellow gone.

Martyn picked up the bag of snow which had been collected outside. He filled part of a pot with the snow and placed the pot on the stove and waited. Slowly the large mound of snow melted, slipping down into the pot as it did so, simmering into water. When the first mound of snow was gone, he added another until the pot was filled with water. Then he poured some of the water into a second pot, added snow and waited for the snow to melt until he had a second pot of water. It took time to get cooking water in the Antarctic.

With his oversized red Swiss army knife, Martyn selected a large potato from the food sack, and cut the potato into small pieces, then added the slices to the boiling water. He diced a chunk of beef, cut up some carrots, and added them to the stew. Within a short time, the other pot was boiling and Martyn added dried soup to the water and stirred. Jim helped with the preparations.

He worked from a numbered food bag for this night. Each bag was numbered and contained a different menu. Each of the first 17 food bags was different to provide variety to our meals. When all 17 food bags would be consumed, we'd start all over with the second set of 17 bags. The second set replicated exactly the first; the third set of 17 was the same as the second. As a result, we planned to consume each recipe three times.

Soon the other members of the expedition gathered in

the tent. A second plywood board had been laid out on other plastic food containers to serve as a dining table. Folding stools had been arranged around the table. Each stool had three aluminum legs and a canvas seat. By properly balancing yourself on the stool, you managed to sit in comfort. Now and then one of us fell over, but that was not to be helped.

At 7:30 p.m. the chow call went out. Those of us—which usually meant me—who had not yet arrived, came into the mess tent to join the others. Each of us had a one-pint plastic measuring cup which served as a bowl for soup, a coffee cup for coffee, a glass for cool drinks, and a dish for meals.

One by one, we passed our cups down to Martyn, who filled the cup with soup. I added a large chunk of butter to the soup, as did most of the others. I could feel the thick soup warm my mouth, throat and stomach. The butter brought a surge of warmth. In Antarctica, you need butter to provide energy against the cold. When the soup was consumed, Martyn filled our cups with stew. A large spoon of vegetables and beef was heaped in my empty mug, and then another spoon and another until the mug was full. I added several large chunks of butter.

Normally a meal this size would send my weight soaring. But the cold and the seven hours of skiing would more than offset the added calories. But I knew I would lose a half pound of weight a day, despite eating all the carbohydrates I could stuff in. Ron took measures of weight loss every week. What surprised me was that they would show that each of us lost not only fat, but protein and muscle as well.

The warm stew filled my stomach and made dinner the second most pleasurable part of the day. The first was sleep. We all looked forward to dinner, for there was no danger of gaining weight. We could eat as we liked, as much as we wished. Actually, we had to eat—for if we did not, we would lack the energy to stay warm and move forward.

Everyone consumed the first bowl and all of us looked forward to second helpings which Martyn divided among us. Besides the soup and the stew, we had small chunks of cheese and crackers. Before and after, we also had available cocoa, hot milk, tea, or coffee with sugar and powdered cream. I usually ate several slices of Swiss cheese.

The heat from the stoves and that of the eleven bodies gradually warmed the mess tent. It felt good to be here, good to be well fed again, good to be together in the off-beat atmosphere.

Martyn asked if there were any problems or suggestions. J.K. had advice. We must be certain to stay together on the trail, he reiterated. Martyn tried to suggest how. Most of us knew that we could not stay together all the time or very well. Shirley read poems.

Someone remarked that the carbon-monoxide warning tab had turned black, indicating that the carbon-monoxide level was at a dangerous level. The poisoning came from the MSR stoves.

But the tablet remained black, so no one paid much attention. If we died of fumes, we would die. There was no way of avoiding the problem, so it was not worth worrying much about.

During the journey down from Patriot Hills, the Teflon runners of the sledges towed by the Ski-Doos had been ripped partway off.

Both sledges were on their sides and would have to be repaired before we continued our journey. Stuart and Mike planned to make the repairs in the morning.

Although the wind was high, I decided to sleep outside once again in my yellow bivouac sack.

After I had climbed into the bag, the wind flapped

against my protective cover, so I buried my head in my red jacket, pulled my pile hat over my ears, and covered my eyes with my airline blindfold. Soon my world was dark and oblivious.

I now lay on an ice sheet 1,500 feet thick. Below the ice was land; to the north was the Ronne Ice Shelf, and at the northern edge of the Ronne shelf lay open water.

Soon I forgot about where I was and I fell asleep, no longer aware of the flapping of my bag or the sharp noise of the polar wind beating against the tents beyond me.

Section 3

THE LONG
SKI JOURNEY
TO THE
POLE

In a 70 m.p.h. polar gust, a team member struggles with his equipment. High winds and fierce Antarctic cold at times forced the ski team to temporarily delay its historic trek and

Top, J. K. Bajaj; below left, Jerry Corr;
below right, Shirley Metz

Top, Alejo Contreras-Steading;
below left, Tori Murden; below right, Stuart Hamilton

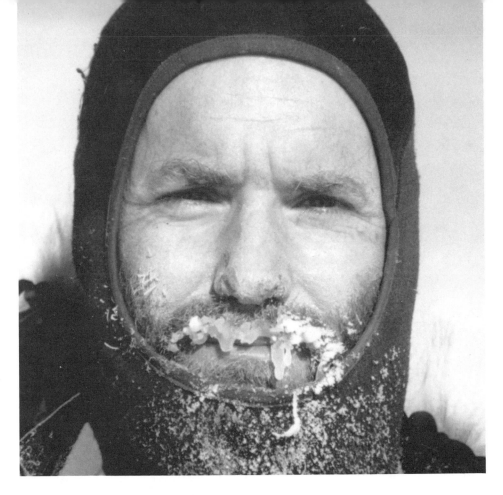

Top, Ron Milnarik; below left,
Jim Williams; below right, Mike Sharp

Top, the new route for the skiers lay step-by-step from the
Ronne Ice Shelf to the South Pole, a distance of 750 miles.
Below, the sastrugi was at times ice-hard and treacherous.

Top, Lewis Nunatak jutted through the ice cap. Below, in a whiteout, skiers set up camp for the night.

Top, a skier packed his sled and readied his equipment.
Below, the team rested seven minutes each hour, their
backs to the wind.

On their pioneering trek, the skiers crossed a vast polar
landscape of perpetual ice and snow.

Top, the Thiel mountains were covered in mist as the expedition took a rest stop. Below, the expedition's tent village sprang up each night on the Antarctic ice.

Top, to celebrate Christmas, a cross of snow was erected in front of the tents. **Below,** each morning, Martyn Williams read from Scott of the Antarctic's diary for that day.

Top, despite high polar winds, the Twin Otter landed to resupply the team. Here, a skier struggled to carry food from the aircraft into the mess tent.

Overleaf: At the South Pole at last: (left to right): J.K. Bajaj, Martyn Williams, Stuart Hamilton, Mike Sharp, Jim Williams, Jerry Corr, Tori Murden, Shirley Metz, Ron Milnarik, Alejo contreras-Steading, and author Joe Murphy

6 / FIRST STEPS
SOUTH

OUR PLAN was to follow the Ellsworth Range south
from the land edge of the Antarctic continent, where it
met the Ronne Ice Shelf. These mountains, ten miles to
the west, would serve as guides for at least the first
week, since the range ran south to nearly parallel our
intended route.

But we could use these guides only if the sun were out
and we were not enveloped in cloud and blinded by
whiteout. Otherwise, we would have to rely on our
compasses.

Navigation would be a major problem.

There are no signposts in Antarctica—no roads, no
rivers, no intersections, nothing to tell you where you
are. Before arriving, I had imagined a great white blank

on the map—a field of white where every feature was indistinguishable from every other.

I later joked to the others: "We can take one camera shot of the landscape and show it a hundred times. The scenery is all the same."

They laughed, recognizing the grain of truth in the humor.

The universal nature of our environment was especially true in *whiteout*, surrounded by fog or cloud, when I could not tell land from sky. I could not see the horizon. My eyes failed to distinguish the waves of snow, the dropoffs, the bumps, the hills and the valleys. In whiteout, it was treacherous to ski.

On whiteout days, I often fell. We all tumbled, landing on the hard surface of the snow with a crack.

But whiteout wasn't the only worry.

The main problem was knowing where we were and knowing where we were going.

When we started the journey at the edge of the Ronne Ice Shelf, a one-degree error in direction would result in a large error at the pole. So knowing our direction precisely was extremely important.

But how to know? That was a major problem for the expedition.

In the year before departure, I had frequently asked myself: *"How could we know where we were? How could we be sure to travel directly to the pole and not angle off to one side or the other?"*

If we angled off, we might bypass the pole, wander into the zone of the unknown—and possibly be lost forever.

I knew that there were several devices we could use to assure the proper direction.

The simplest device to use was a compass. By simply

pointing our compasses south, we would assure our general direction. But was that enough?

Theoretically, the compass was easy to use. Applying the compass in practice was another matter.

The second day out clarified the difficulty. We had been following the Ellsworth Range to our right, a low-lying series of peaks ten miles away. The range ran generally north-south. By paralleling the peaks, we assured a course that took us toward the pole.

But the use of the Ellsworths as a guide depended on our ability to see them. Occasionally on the first day out, the mountains slid from sight, either because our route dipped below a rise or because a low-lying cloud obscured the range.

The disappearance of the Ellsworths was not critical that first day since dead ahead was a nunatak that marked our course back to the Patriot Hills. Patriot Hills would be our first stop south on the route to the pole. By lining up on the nunatak, we assured a correct course.

Moreover, the nunatak was rarely obscured by clouds. Consequently, keeping the right direction was not difficult.

Slowly the line of skiers formed and headed for the first nunatak. Our movements varied. Sometimes we skied abreast, strung out in a wide flanking movement. We moved this way when the objective was clearly before us, as it was now.

Then the clouds moved in and visibility dimmed. We shifted tactics, moving into a single file, a thin line of skiers all decked out in red parkas. Behind us, we towed our sleds.

The line weaved back and forth in slow motion as each skier searched out the easier contours in the wild waves of snow. Sometimes I could see only the back of the skier ahead.

At other times the whole line was in sight. This happened when the lead skier curved sharply right or left to avoid a particularly large crest of snow.

Though we had promised each other to keep together, to remain equally spaced like a squad of infantry troops on patrol, we generally failed to stay in a straight line. The lead skier often got far ahead and the last skiers lagged far behind.

"We are behaving like a *yo-yo*," Martyn complained. "We must stay more together."

"Yo-yo" might have been the right word. It certainly described the difficulty. But when Martyn took the lead to solve the problem, he only worsened it.

He was such a fast skier, with his constant shuffle, almost like a dancer on skis, that the tail of the line stretched even further back and the lead took off like a sprinter.

It was *no use*. Despite periodic remonstrating by Martyn, or J.K., or by someone else, we failed to stick together.

The line of skiers stretched and strained like an ungainly team of horses whose harness was made of elastic, not leather. The bands of resolve were simply torn asunder by the rough terrain, and the unequal strength and speed of the skiers.

We skied at unequal spacing and there was little that could be done about it. The constant swaying of the line, the stretching of the red suits fore and aft, was resolved at the end of each hour as we came together to rest.

The rest stops, made to give us a chance to breathe, started out at 15 minutes, but were later cut to 7 minutes to keep us from cooling down too much in the high wind.

When I stopped, took off my mitts, and sat on top of

my sled to rest my weary legs, my body gradually cooled. I knew the trick was to stop long enough to catch my breath, restore my strength, or relieve myself before the next stretch of skiing.

At the rest stops, the straggling line of skiers reconsolidated at a single point. Then it surged forth again and slowly dispersed.

Seen from above, the scene must have appeared a strange sight, the nine red dots moving out in a lengthening line, weaving slightly, occasionally moving abreast, and then coming together again at the end of each hour.

This stringing out and then reformation occurred punctually, hour after hour. As it did, the person in the lead changed on the order of Martyn, who always designated who was to go first.

"Would you like to lead?" he would ask the next person in a polite request.

Eventually, Tori started the day, then Ron, and then others, one by one, each with a slightly different pace. The particular pace affected how much we stretched or swayed, how much we parted. This movement, back and forth, was a good part of our day.

It took up our thoughts. If the person ahead moved far ahead, you tried to catch up and the energy expended catching up was more than you otherwise might spend. So the line itself, its machinations, its spacing, stretched and tugged at the energy each of us put out.

If I fell behind now, where would I be at the end? This thought recurred time and time again.

Such rumblings raced through my mind, especially in the first two weeks when I was out of shape and not sure whether I could sustain the effort required to get to the pole.

The navigational problem caused by the weaving line did not become clear until the second day out. On that day, the nunatak that had guided our course disappeared to the rear behind a rise in the snow.

A second rise, a long gentle swell in the snow, rose to the west, obscuring the features of the Ellsworth range. When the Ellsworth mountains disappeared, we had nothing but the compass to guide us.

In the days before the expedition, I had imagined walking over a flat, featureless plain holding a compass before me, arm outstretched. I imagined holding the compass high enough to sight along the hairline so I could see the white part of the needle in the mirror so as to give me an accurate bearing.

But a flat plain is different from erratic waves of snow. This is much more like sailing a boat at sea with no more than a compass to guide you. The wind and the waves continually force the boat slightly off course, this way and that. How can one hold the right course? I wondered.

The sun glanced off distant waves of snow. By picking a distant point, I could take its bearing and head for it.

But as I crossed one wave of snow after the other, I lost sight of the speck of light that was guiding me. I'd confuse it with another speck, or the speck would sink below the surface long enough that I could not find it.

Then, if I were lucky enough to find it again, I would reach it and have to look for another.

Sometimes, a cloud passed over and the speck of light disappeared, or no patch of snow became sunstruck. Everything seemed to look like every other: a land of dull-gray-white featureless snow.

Holding a line of course now seemed impossible.

It was largely guesswork. Mere guesswork. I pondered anew how we could reach the pole with such a lack of precision.

This discouraging state of affairs deteriorated further

late in the second day. The low cloud that faced us moved in slowly but unremittingly.

Soon the features ahead were obscured by a white mist. The horizon line disappeared. It became impossible to tell what was snow and what was sky. The obscurity soon expanded to the left and to the right of us. Quickly, we became enveloped in the mist.

Even my skis disappeared from sight. The sharp folds in the waves of snow became a flat white in my poor vision.

Martyn had planned for this problem and had worked out a means of navigation. The lead person was to hold the compass course. The rest of us, following in single file, were to keep a straight line.

The last person in line, so the theory went, would tell the lead to move left or right whenever the line became crooked. By keeping a straight line, we could hold a course due south.

Practice proved more difficult than theory. The yo-yo tendency, the weaving back and forth, and the meandering from side to side, all made this theoretical procedure difficult to accomplish.

"Keep the line," Martyn shouted.

"Bear *right*," someone else yelled at the lead.

"Not that much right—*a little left*."

I could barely hear. It was hard to see. My goggles kept fogging up. I stumbled on the hard waves of snow in the whiteness.

Is this what Limbo is like? I wondered. Not knowing where you are, where you are going, or when, even if, you will get there, is disconcerting, particularly when you cannot even tell up from down.

Our pace slowed. We stumbled. Someone ahead of me fell. Everyone behind had to stop while the fallen figure pulled himself or herself up. The lead skiers moved further ahead.

If we had much more whiteout like this, I realized, we would lose our way.

It was a tortuous method of navigation and travel. We made slow progress—not enough to reach the pole before the first week of February.

Even that early date might be too late to permit escape.

The skiers ahead continued to stumble. Three times I fell. Three times I worked myself back to the erect position. In the bad light it was difficult to get up.

I could not tell which way was up.

I pushed up in one direction, then discovered that I was at an angle to the vertical. I fell back in surprise, then tried again.

Where is *south* became where is *up*? *Down* was easy enough to find, however.

What a miserable day. *We will never make it like this*, I thought.

In the distance, a patch of sunlight appeared. The narrow beam of light danced back and forth under a hole in the clouds.

Slowly, the opening enlarged. Soon a long streak of light lit the snow. The heavy fog began to thin and disperse, gradually losing its vigor. Far off, to the left front, another strand of sun appeared like a beacon to the lost.

We could see.

"Bear right of the nunatak," Martyn advised. "By about 30 degrees." The tight line of skiers loosened. Soon we were skiing abreast.

No longer were we lost.

The waves of snow reappeared. Shadow and light revealed the troubled terrain beneath our skis.

Patriot Hills came into view slowly. Alejo, who was farsighted, spotted one of the Twin Otters of the Chilean Air Force that was stationed within a few hundred yards of our base camp.

On this generally flat terrain, visibility was limited to ten miles—unless a mountain range beckoned from afar. That was the limit of sight of a six-foot person looking as far as he or she could.

Beyond that the terrain remained a mystery. Sometimes, a slight roll in the land, a long swell of snow, allowed you to see a little further, or kept you from seeing as far. We were often in one of these situations of extended, or restricted vision. Generally, vision was restricted.

In addition to our compass, we had an electronic device for determining where we were. It was a satellite navigation device called a SATNAV.

This marvel was supposed to depict our position within one meter. It relied on one of the five satellites that passed over the South Pole at this time of year.

Ships commonly used SATNAVs to determine their position in the ocean. The device was far more accurate than using a sextant to take a position by stars. You could fix your position with unbelievable accuracy.

But there was a hitch. The SATNAV didn't always work properly. If the battery ran down, or the electronics were off, or if something else occurred, this extraordinary electronic unit didn't work.

Ours didn't work now. We weren't getting the right readings. We knew where we were, but the SATNAV said we were somewhere else far off.

When we got back to base at Patriot Hills, Dick Smith was there. As the head of *Australian Geographic,* Smith was an electrical engineer by training. He had done a lot of work with computers. Also, he knew something about Antarctica, having just completed the first circumnavigation of the continent by air with Giles Kershaw, a pilot for China Airlines and the leading Antarctica bush pilot.

I watched Smith put the wonder on the camp dining

table. Carefully he studied the instructions and started pushing the buttons. He fidgeted with it for over an hour. There was not much time to get the thing working, since we would leave tomorrow for the pole and Smith and Kershaw planned to fly out this afternoon. Both Stuart and Martyn made periodic inquiries, each with a slightly worried tone of voice.

Finally, Smith looked up.

"You're missing a program. This device is meant for ships at sea level. At the pole you'll be *9,000 feet above* sea level. That's the problem."

Smith did get the machine working, however, in a rough-hand sort of way. How long it would hold any degree of accuracy was another matter. We knew that the closer we got to the pole, which meant the higher our altitude above sea level, the lower would be the accuracy of this supposedly perfect locator. We would be off—and we had no way of knowing how far off.

For a time, anyway, we had the mountains to guide us. We could follow them when the weather was clear.

We had a rough-drawn map of the area that gave the location of the ranges, the isolated peaks, and the blue ice fields as well as the longitudes and latitudes of these features.

How accurate the maps were was also another problem.

Nunataks we saw did not appear on the maps. Nunataks that appeared on the maps sometimes failed to appear on the surface of the snow.

So we had guides—but even these were uncertain.

The route from base camp was clear. We headed directly to the mountain over the patch of blue ice that served as a runway for the DC-4.

A long snow ramp led directly from the ice, ending in a saddle. Beyond the saddle stretched two ranges: on the right, the Ellsworth, true mountains rising several thousand feet above the snow. On the left rose the Patriot Hills, a much more sculptured range of peaks.

Our course lay directly ahead between the two parallel ranges. Now there was no need to stay together, no requirement for maintaining a line, no cause for a compass course.

The mountains told us clearly where we were and where we had to go.

Jerry and I had started first. On this terrain, I carried my skis, since it was easier walking. I had on the big Canadian military boots, boots large enough to allow my big toe to recuperate from the infection that plagued it.

The others were strung out behind, quite far in the distance. As I paced along, I saw no one, for Jerry was far to my left and a short distance ahead.

It was good to be on our way, good to see the mountains to my right and left, and especially good not to be in a single file. Now I felt more alone and free.

I relished the space and not having to worry about tight grouping. I felt joyful in my relative solitude.

I knew of no immediate fear and felt no pangs of anxiety.

But as it turned out, my confidence was premature.

7 / THE FALL

WE INTENDED TO MOVE OUT EARLY, but it was not until 11:00 a.m. that we finally departed. The day was clear and cold, with a light wind that gradually rose to 15 m.p.h.

We were moving well, but finding that regulating our body heat was a constant problem. At the start of the day, my hands were frozen from taking down the tent and packing the gear. Twenty minutes into the run, my hands had warmed. Soon, I began to sweat.

After each break, the pattern was the same: initial freezing, frozen hands, then warmth, and finally sweat. By the end of the day, a heavy crust of ice had formed on my mask and on the outside of my pile mitt liners, even though the nylon shell was dry. I never solved the problem completely.

The snow was hard and tricky, making it easy to fall. I

was careful to avoid slipping on the hard spots and not tripping my skis on the snow ridges, which would result in my being thrown to the ground. I was not always successful.

After a few hours of frustration, I took off the skis, hoisted them over my shoulder, and switched to walking.

My infected toe had not healed, so I was glad to wear my Canadian military boots. Though the boots were heavy, they were warm and roomy, just what I needed for my toe. To use them, my three-pin bindings had to be removed from my skis and replaced by plastic Berwin bindings.

Initially, the change was a relief. But after a time, the hard snow became soft, my boots sank in and plodding along in heavy boots became burdensome. I tried to avoid the soft areas by watching the snow pattern carefully, noting where a hard glaze covered the surface or wind-packed ridges angled in various directions.

The constant searching for hard snow began to take all my concentration.

On the seventh day came the weather we feared most: whiteout. As I rolled out of my bag, I saw that the sky was completely overcast and there was a light wind. The temperature had remained the same overnight, still 12 degrees Fahrenheit, but it was now dropping.

The whiteout was not welcome. Wind was preferable to whiteout, for we could move reasonably well with the protection of our Scott ski masks, which covered the entire face. Without the masks, we would be in dire straits.

I was beginning to have more problems on the trail. In addition to my infected and painful toe, I found I had a large red sore on my groin, which became highly inflamed. I worried that I had acquired some dreaded social disease from new unwashed underwear I'd gotten just before leaving home. I knew that I had not acquired it in any other way. To cure the sore, I applied zinc oxide.

Arriving at breakfast last, I gulped down my oatmeal with relish. After that, I drank cocoa, which I preferred to tea or coffee. Jerry and Shirley had already cut the cheese and salami. I took one piece of each, made peanut butter and jelly sandwiches and added pieces of dried fruit, and a chocolate bar, and stuffed the lot into my plastic bag for lunch. Mike had filled the steel Thermos bottles, and I added Tang to mine. I wanted to drink as much as I could to prevent possible dehydration.

The sky remained overcast and the fog lay ahead in the distance. Ron took the lead, since Tori, who usually led the first hour, had a bad Achille's tendon.

Trying to hold a straight course in the fog was trying and difficult. Distant blocks of snow, which sparkled in the sunlight, were now hidden.

Goggles frosted, and sweat condensed on the lens. I had to take off my glasses to see, but nearsightedness kept me from seeing very far.

Ron held a steady pace for two hours on a course of 220 degrees. We were headed for the Pirrit Hills and beyond them for the Thiel Mountains, which we hoped to reach by Christmas, just two weeks away.

When I took the lead at noon, I was glad I'd switched back to my Telemark boots. They were steadier than the loose military boots and the plastic Berwin bindings. To make the Asolo boots roomy enough, I had put my climbing Aveolite liners inside, instead of the normal liner, and I wore only a single pair of wool socks.

Skiing in a whiteout and at the front of the line is like wandering through a cloud where nothing is visible. When you're leading, you cannot watch the snow below you. You cannot see the dips and valleys under your feet, but have to concentrate on the signs ahead.

My goggles soon fogged. I finally took them off to improve the view, relying on my glacier glasses alone. To make matters worse, in the humid air, my temperature rose and my polypropylene underwear became soaking wet.

Despite the fog, we moved steadily, stopping briefly each hour. By mid-afternoon, the sun appeared and the overcast changed to long streams of cirrus clouds. Everyone felt relieved.

We again could see the Ellsworth Range behind us and Mount Goodwin ahead in the distance. The view was magnificent.

The skiing remained hard and slippery, however, and I fell in the sastrugi, flat on my face.

The next day was Sunday, the day for our medical tests. We each placed a dip stick into our urine; the results could be sent to Lise to test whether we were burning fat or muscle. We also used a complicated machine that took our blood pressure. You rolled your sleeve up, attached a Velcro strap to your arm, pushed a button, waited until the air pressure in the strap inflated it, and then read the digital result.

Before turning in, I taped the cracks on the tips of my fingers and checked the sore on my crotch. The rash was better. So was my infected toe. Though bedtime wasn't until 11:00, I dozed off immediately and slept without waking until morning.

We marched toward the beautiful summits of the Pirrit Hills, and we crossed the milestone of 81 degrees south latitude. It was a happy moment, for we had only 9 degrees left to cover.

In a sense, it seemed odd that we should celebrate crossing the 81st parallel, a one-degree advance. But it was our first milestone and it had taken a long time to reach, much longer than it should have taken.

As we started out the next morning, the distant peaks of Mount Goodwin were barely visible; they became more discernible with each passing hour.

The sastrugi were unusually rough today, like the ocean frozen in violent waves, chaotic, unpredictable torrents of white, often high enough to toss you flat on your back. Every day someone fell, but today we all fell, even Martyn, who fell twice. No bones had been broken, nothing that might stop our progress. But we were all concerned about injury.

I had to adjust to the crests and valleys with each stride. If one yard ran flat, the next curved left, right, under, or down—sometimes a foot, occasionally five. As the wax of my skis wore off, they slid unpredictably this way and that. I had a horrible time of it.

It is frequently the unexpected event that alters the course of action, or spells doom to an enterprise. Had I been asked what event might end our expedition to the South Pole, I could have named several likely candidates—whiteout, failure of transport, impassable crevasses, unmitigated cold, or unforgiving terrain.

But none of these had the impact that this entirely unforeseen event did. We nearly lost our leader.

We had passed the Ellsworth range, climbed the gradual snow ramp that led to the plateau beyond the range, and were making good time.

The day was generally clear. No whiteout obscured our way. The hard waves of snow were occasionally formidable, but not unsurmountable. They were nothing that could not be ascended or circumvented.

We alternated the lead, took our usual seven-minute breaks, and then continued on. We took 15 minutes for lunch, sitting on our sleds, backs to the wind. The sun slid around the land with its usual predictability, moving to our left as the day moved on. By our watches, the only measure of time we had, it was mid-afternoon. The peaks of the Ellsworths had disappeared.

We climbed a stiff rise toward Mount Goodwin, a peak that had been directly in our line of march for most of the day. This isolated peak, this nunatak, rose slowly as we approached. Its wind-scarred silhouette became more and more detailed as we neared its base.

Jerry and I were in the lead as we slowly wound our way up the slope. The sun slanted across the snow from the west. The surface beneath our skis was slippery, partly hard snow, partly blue ice.

Suddenly, I slipped backward once, then again and again.

The third time I fell. The hard ice jammed against my shoulder.

In my difficulty, I barely heard Jerry's voice. *"They want us to stop,"* he shouted. *"Something's happened!"*

I turned carefully around. The others were strung out behind us. Martyn came up first.

"Snowmobiles coming," he said, breathlessly. I scanned the horizon, but could see nothing. Then, I spotted an object in the distance.

"It's too early," someone added. "The snowmobiles are not due until 5." I glanced at my watch. It was barely 2:00 p.m.

I looked for the two snowmobiles, but I saw only a single machine hauling a single sledge.

Stewart stopped a ways off, then climbed up to where we were. "The sledge *broke*," he blurted out.

"Again?" Martyn was clearly frustrated.

"The sastrugi were too rough," the driver apologized. "I kept watching for the high waves of snow, but I didn't see one until it was too late. The sledge has got to be repaired."

"We'll wait here," Martyn replied.

Slowly Stuart headed back down the hill. When he reached the sledge, he began unloading the duffels. He had brought what we needed to camp: our duffels and the tents.

After he left, we had the prospect of two or three hours to wait with nothing to do. Several of us had pulled up our sleds, and sat resting, backs to the wind.

To wait and do nothing was ominous. In a short time, we would be frozen.

"Let's go," Martyn said suddenly, heading off toward Mount Goodwin.

He sensed the need to keep warm, to be active while we waited for the sledge to be repaired.

Mount Goodwin lay directly to the west and north. Its eastern flank rose 2,000 feet above us, a single peak with rock walls. To the north lay a small subsidiary peak connected to the main peak by a saddle.

Between us and Mount Goodwin ran a river of blue ice, a glacier that dropped off to the north and descended steeply 400 feet.

I could not see the bottom.

Martyn began skiing across the glacier ice to the snowfield beyond. .

The rest of us, anxious to get warm, followed—all but Tori and Jerry. Jerry headed off for the main peak.

My skis slid on the ice. A slip or a long skid would cause me to hurtle over the crest and crash down the glacier.

For an instant, I thought I would go over. Quickly, I jammed my ski poles into the ice and caught myself. When I reached the snow, I sighed with relief.

Then I followed Martyn's lead. We climbed the slope on our skis to the subsidiary rock peak, cached our skis and then headed for the summit of the peak. A rock buttress jutted about 30 feet above the snow, forming the peak.

When I reached the corner of the rock peak, I could

see what lay beyond on the north side: a smooth, white, almost icy surface that swept down on the north. It curved over like the upper surface of a large ball.

I could not see the slope, for it dropped too precipitously. Far below was the flat field of blue ice that ran north for a half mile. The smooth slope I stood on swept down to the glacier. Below, to the left, was a long, low moraine running north that divided the blue glacier in half.

I had followed Martyn around the corner of the rock. I watched him examine the surface and then scramble back over the rock in the direction of the cached skis. Shirley found a nook in the rock where she sat with some protection from the blasting wind. I joined her.

In a few minutes Martyn reappeared, followed by Jim, Alejo, and eventually Ron.

"You're not going to ski on this?" I cried. *"You'll kill yourself."*

Martyn said nothing as he slipped into his skinny skating skis.

My God, I thought, he doesn't even have steel edges. Those skis won't hold on this glassy surface.

Martyn shoved off, then tried a few telemark turns on the gentle upper slope. Expert skier that he was, his turns worked reasonably well.

But the edges of his skis slipped slightly.

Jim followed. Slowly they glided over the crest of the hill.

Then I saw nothing, only the bright shiny surface of the crest of the hill and the pale blue of the glacier far below.

The strong wind whipped across my face, chilling my body. There was not a sound.

I walked carefully to the edge of the hill in the wind, and looked down. I saw no one, only the pale blue ice. Not a sign of Martyn or Jim.

"Martyn," I called, now growing alarmed. *"Jim."*

There was no answer.

I sensed something was very wrong.

The turns at first had seemed easy. Martyn had no difficulty on the upper slope executing a perfect telemark. The slope to right was steeper, but still looked all right.

Jim had descended to the left, making turns easily. He reached the bottom without difficulty.

As Martyn began the next turn on the steeper section, he felt one ski slip.

Then the second ski went out from under him.

He lost control and started sliding downward. The surface was too slick to hold.

He felt his body hurtling down the icy slope.

The bottom curved out. If he could slide out, there might be no harm. There was hope.

Then, Martyn saw a large rock directly in his path. Terrible fleeting thoughts flashed through his mind.

Jim had looked up to watch Martyn slip, fall and then start sliding downward.

The rock was in Martyn's path.

Jim watched Martyn accelerate and rush toward a large rock. He barely missed the big rock, but hit some small ones.

Martyn came to a stop. Jim waited for him to rise.

Martyn lay still.

For ten minutes, he did not move.

Jim laboriously climbed up to where Martyn lay. The body was still, but he was breathing. Slowly Martyn came to.

He was *alive*.

We waited a long time at the top of the hill. Ron had gone down to investigate. After some minutes he returned.

But his silence seemed strange.

Finally, he said: "There's nothing to worry about."

"What does that *mean?*" I asked.

But I received no reply.

A head appeared over the crest. It was *Martyn.*

He seemed to be moving very slowly. Then Jim appeared.

"*Are you okay?*" I asked Martyn, when he reached us. He did not answer my question.

"*How's Joe?*" he asked in return. That's how he inevitably greeted me.

Then he said nothing more. He slowly trudged past.

Finally, a few days later, I saw the bruise. Martyn's ribs and hip were an ugly black and blue. But nothing was broken.

He was in severe pain. Ron gave him drugs to relieve the suffering.

It had been a narrow escape. For him.

And for all of us.

8 / ON THE TRAIL

THE DAY WAS MISERABLE, with a harsh wind
from the south. We struggled against the wind and the
hard, swirling sastrugi for seven hours. Our skis
slipped, slithered, and slid every which way, placing a
constant strain on our feet, ankles, legs, arms, hands,
and brains.

At each break, when I took off my skis and rewaxed
the bottoms, my fingers nearly froze. During our stops,
I shivered in the wind, and even a cup of hot tea or
cocoa didn't help much. I always was eager to be off
again—so I could generate enough heat to warm my
body against the constant chill.

The cold was awful. My goggles fogged, my body was
chilled, and even my spine shivered at the end of every
break and at the start of each new leg of the journey.

The harsh conditions prompted my doubts. Why had I

come on this cold, hellish journey? *Would I be strong enough to keep up?*

Sometimes, when the pace seemed too fast, I cursed the pacesetter. I had calculated the number of steps we required in order to reach the pole—*three million.* That enormous number was almost too much for my mind to contemplate.

Was I insane? I counted the progress I had completed hour after hour, day after day, week after week. *When would it end?*

By this time, I had endured only about a week and a half of skiing.

"If I can make the first two weeks, I can make the course," I kept repeating.

But I was not certain whether I really believed myself.

Now, in full harness, I regretted my lack of training. The few walks I had made around the lake at home were clearly insufficient.

What's more, it was evident I had not worked out enough in the fall after my collarbone had mended.

Would Martyn discover my poor condition? If he discovered it, what would he say?

"Well, Joe, I don't think you're up to it. You won't make it all the way to the pole."

I imagined Martyn concluding, *"It's best you take the Twin Otter out. You're not in good enough shape. We will be going too fast for you to keep up."*

These imaginary conversations plagued me. They echoed in my mind in the loneliness of this Antarctic wasteland. I disliked the unending effort and having to endure the solitude. I hated the harsh wind and bitter cold, mile after mile.

I tried to be philosophical. I had learned that total misery, when it is over, often breeds happiness, particularly when the result is success. I did not find much comfort in philosophy, however.

Despite my grumblings, by the time we reached camp, we had made 14 miles in a harsh wind, a remarkable achievement.

At dinner, we recovered after a very tough day. Spirits were high. We found we had come within one day of 82 degrees south and within three days of the Martin Hills.

Feeling good when I returned to my tent, I actually was glad to be here again.

But later on, the gale tore at our tent so loudly that I could not hear Jerry talk over the noise. The beating of the polar wind kept me awake much of the long, restless night.

By morning the wind was growing stronger, 30 miles per hour gusting to 40. It drove the snow and brought wind chill.

The wind was so high that we decided to wait for it to die down before moving out, hoping to forestall the possibility of frostbite and the complications that could ensue. To prevent the gusts from tearing down our sleeping tent, we increased the height of the wall on the windward side from two to four feet.

By noon, there had been no letup in the blast of air from the south. Soon, four-foot-high drifts had piled up between the tents. The drifts were so hard that my boots made no dent in the surface.

Pinned down by the gale, we retreated to our shelters, crawled into our sleeping bags, and relished the chance to rest. It was the first day we did not have to ski and we made the most of it.

In the mess tent, Martyn and Mike debated the reasons for the SATNAV errors and found they could not agree. We could pick up five satellites that passed over the

South Pole, but each satellite gave a different reading, and the errors were disturbing.

The danger was that we might not find the South Pole.

"The cause of the error," Stuart reiterated, "is our elevation. The instrument is calibrated for ships at sea level, and it won't work this high. That's the reason for the error."

I listened until the details became too great for concentration.

During this time of enforced rest caused by the storm, we talked of our homes and of our past. Today, I learned something of our Chilean representative, Alejo. At age 37, he was Chile's most experienced traveler to the Antarctic. He had spent more time here than any of his countrymen.

I looked at the pictures of his wife and young son.

"My son won't know me when I return," he said, with a sigh. "He is too young; I am absent too long."

Wind, wind, *wind!* The blast of cold swept down from the south and continued to blow at 20 to 30 miles per hour. The snow lines were deep.

Our tent was gradually sinking, and my great red duffel and pack were buried. Alejo's Chilean flag flew straight out in the blast of air.

We won't go today, I thought. *If the wind doesn't let up, we will never make it.*

The morning gathering was somber. Jerry, ever anxious to move on, thought we might walk instead of ski, "moving slowly." These were stark words coming from him. Shirley felt the same.

"We'll see," Martyn said.

Ron countered, "The wind speed is only 10 to 20 miles per hour." He had been reading his flimsy anemometer.

"We won't rely on that," said Martyn. "We'll make a visual check."

Martyn disappeared for a moment, and when he returned, the verdict was not to go.

"The danger of frostbite is too great," he concluded. "It's not worth it. We'll check again at 12:00 noon and again at 1:00 p.m."

Not till late afternoon did the wind subside; by then it was much too late to move out.

So we spent another day of talking, resting, and reading.

The cold, penetrating my boots from the floor of the mess tent, was so intense that I retreated to my sleeping bag, where I attempted to warm up my feet. I was worried particularly about my big toe, which had lost all sensation.

It took four hours in the warmth of my sleeping bag to revive my feet.

Every morning after breakfast, Martyn pulled out his copy of Robert Falcon Scott's famous Antarctic diary and read the passage for the day.

On the morning of December 5, Martyn read to us what the Antarctic explorer had written on December 5. He was describing his attempt to reach the South Pole for the first time.

As I listened to the words, to the vibrant sounds of Scott of the Antarctic's clear and graphic prose, I marveled at his ability to write so well under such adverse conditions:

"Tuesday, December 5. Camp 30. Noon. We awoke this morning to a raging, howling blizzard. The blows we have had hitherto have lacked the very fine powdery snow—that especial feature of the blizzard. Today we have it fully developed. After a minute or two in the open, one is covered from head to foot. The temperature is high, so that what falls or drives against one sticks. The ponies—heads, tails, legs, and all parts not protected by their rugs—are covered with ice; the animals are standing, deep in snow, the sledges are almost covered, and huge drifts (are) above the tents. We have had breakfast, rebuilt the walls, and are now again in our bags. One cannot see the next tent, let alone the land. What on earth does such weather mean at this time of the year? It is more than our share of ill fortune, I think, but the luck may turn yet. I doubt if any party could travel in such weather, even with the wind; certainly, no one could travel against it."

Later on that day, he wrote:

"**11 p.m.** It has blown all day with quite the greatest snowfall I remember. The drifts about the tents are simply huge. The temperature was +27 degrees this forenoon, and rose to +31 degrees in the afternoon, at which time the snow melted as it fell on anything but the snow, and, as a consequence, there are pools of water on clothes, night boots, etc.; water drips from the tent poles and door, lies on the floor cloth, soaks the sleeping bags, and makes everything pretty wretched..."

The next day was no better. Again Scott put it graphically. As he did, my mind turned back to 1911 and I tried to imagine what it had been like then:

"**Wednesday, December 6,** Camp 30. Noon. Miserable, utterly miserable. We have camped in the 'Slough of Despond.' The tempest rages with unabated violence. The temperature has gone to +33 degrees; everything in the tent is soaking. People returning from the outside look exactly as though they had been in a heavy shower of rain. They drip pools on the floorcloth. The snow is steadily climbing higher about the walls, ponies, tents and sledges. The ponies look utterly desolate. Oh, but this is too crushing, and we are only 12 miles from the Glacier. A hopeless feeling descends on one and is hard to fight off..."

Every morning we listened to these words. Every day,

I thought back about what had been read and I tried to compare it to what we were experiencing.

Of course, we were on a different route to the pole—hundreds of miles from where Scott had been. We had modern equipment, sleeping bags that were impervious to water, boots that did not soak up wet, clothing that was much lighter, tents that kept out the snow and the moisture. More important, the air was dry.

But in other respects, it was the same—the same eternal white, the same high wind and hard sastrugi, the same monotony, the same pressing on each day against harsh elements.

I felt an affinity to Scott and to his party; I felt close to him. But this closeness was a cause for worry.

I hoped we would not end as he and his party of five had—alone, without food, without water, and ultimately, frozen in the Antarctic ice.

I had become accustomed to my black sleeping bag. The dark color soaked up the warm radiation of the sun, the red silken liner gave the impression of heat, and my dense yellow Ensolite foam pad had became comfortable.

After stopping for camp and crawling in, it usually took only 20 minutes for the heat from my body to warm the bag. By early morning, I was hot and wet from perspiration and had to pull off my long-underwear pants and socks so I could sleep with my bare legs against the bag. By then, the warmth and coziness of the sleeping bag were complete; I basked in comfort. Although the bag had at first felt cramped and small, it now seemed large and roomy.

The Kelty tent was a new design and ideal for our purpose: resistant to the wind, easy to erect, warm in the sun when the wind was not blasting, and long enough to accommodate two of us and our equipment. But it was barely high enough for me to sit up in.

The tent had two front doors, ventilated on either side with screening to allow air to circulate. It also had a screen-like cloth rack above my head that I used to dry out my mitts and socks.

When the air quieted, I opened the vents to bring in fresh air. Since we had repaired the pole, the tent held up. The zippers hadn't snapped, and there were only a few tears in the outside snowflaps.

Tonight, after two hours of storm and wind—and now breathless silence—the tent walls were taut under the strain of packed snow. The fierce yellow of the sun gave a strange glow to the white walls and white ceiling of the tent.

The next day, the wind remained calm, but little could be seen in the whiteout that followed. After two days of rest and forced inactivity, we were eager to get going.

The landscape reflected the aftermath of two days and nights of 50 m.p.h. winds. The sastrugi were rough, as hard as ice. The clouds were low; visibility was less than 100 feet. We could not see the sharp ridges or the treacherous valleys below our skis.

My glasses fogged up so much that I was forced to discard them and ski with goggles only. I could barely see.

The lead skier headed south almost by instinct, carrying a radio turned on, so Martyn could make corrections from the rear —until the radios went dead.

We wandered along in a single line, slowly and unsteadily, worried that the snowmobiles would not be able to find us. To reduce this chance, we placed cairns every 15 minutes, but the light was so flat that even the cairns were nearly invisible. The white markers would be very difficult to find on white snow in white fog.

Skiing became so treacherous that J.K. and I took off our skis, tied them to our faithful little sleds, and walked.

We had been on the trail for 17 days, 15 since leaving Patriot Hills.

Our fuel was running low, food was in short supply, and we had finished the numbered packages of daily stores. We had to make do with scrounging from the extra supplies carried for emergency.

The shortage of snowmobile fuel and stove fuel—essentials for forward movement, making water, and cooking—was more of a problem.

Jerry opened one of the old food bags to see what remained. I watched him pull out a few tea bags and some old oatmeal packs.

Carefully, he placed a tea bag in his large plastic cup, picked up the steel flask of water and poured the steaming water over the shrunken tea bag.

"Butter?" he inquired.

"It's gone," someone said.

I reached for the same discarded food bag and managed to find a packet of oatmeal.

Slowly, I poured the hot water over the meal. The water trickled down, and as it did so, the oatmeal began to puff up. I stirred the mixture and soon the cup was filled. Jerry found a pack of sugar in the discarded bag and I poured it over the meal.

The morsels made me yearn for more. But none was to be had.

Outside, a light wind played across the snow. The sound of the flaps of the next tent grew louder. The weather looked ominous.

"I hope Henry can land today," Martyn said. His words were more hope than certainty. "We're near the bottom of the barrel."

Henry was back at Patriot Hills with the Twin Otter. The food required for the next leg of the journey was there, also.

Originally, we had planned to have four air drops, but

conditions had thwarted that plan. Since we'd run through our food supply and were living off emergency rations and leftovers, we needed a resupply soon.

It wasn't only food we were short of. There wasn't enough fuel either, particularly white gas for the stoves. We needed white gas to cook meals. More important, we needed it to make water. Though there was frozen water everywhere, without heat to turn snow into water, we would have nothing to drink in this white, arid desert.

The Twin Otter was equipped for flying in Antarctica. The twin-prop plane could fly on a single engine, land in a high wind, start in temperatures of 18 degrees below, navigate at low levels across barren snow, and land on snow or blue ice.

Yet there were certain maneuvers the plane could not do. It could not land in low visibility. It could not land if the surface was too rough.

Most of what we saw was too rough. As I looked at the high sastrugi, I thought: not even a Twin Otter could set down here. The broken surface would trash the skis or break the struts.

Henry Perk, the pilot, was Swiss, a former Canadian Mountain Holidays ski guide. He had many years flying this craft in Antarctica.

But even for Henry, there were limits.

The day started out like any other, except for the wind. Perversely, it still blew higher than normal.

We moved slowly through the snow. For the first time, we crossed level snow and flat terrain—a place where the Twin Otter could set down.

At first the sky was only partly clouded, but then fog moved in. A good place to land, I thought, but not with the low ceiling.

The easy skiing became difficult. Then the weather changed again as it did again and again in Antarctica.

The windspeed picked up, passed 20 knots, climbed to over 30 knots, and started to gust at more than 40 knots.

The lead skier was buffeted by winds. Winds racked the rest of the line. I tried to stay directly behind the skier ahead, but it was difficult to do so.

The drifts had become hard and high. The waves of snow kept the line turning and twisting as each of us sought more secure footing. When the person ahead of me moved out of alignment even a little, a blast of air jolted me.

By 3:30 in the afternoon, the wind was gusting to 50 knots. To keep moving ahead, I had to jam my poles into the hard snow and lean forward.

Then the wind increased again.

The skier ahead of me slipped back.

He could make no progress.

The next thing I knew, I also was being pushed back by the gusts. The wind caught me—and my skis slithered backward. I nearly fell on top of my little sled.

"We'll have to stop," Martyn finally decided. "The wind's too strong."

Indeed, it *was*.

Today, the Twin Otter was to come—but could it land in this gale?

No chance, I thought. *Not in this strong wind.*

The snowmobiles arrived, as if by intuition, and we laid out camp. It would be a camp with tents, but with little in the way of food or fuel. For those essentials, we awaited the arrival of the supply plane.

The wind continued to rise. Jerry and I pitched our tent in a howling gale.

The wind beat the flaps of the tent terribly, producing a sound like machine-gun fire. I thought the wind would tear out the tent stakes. As usual, we pitched the tent with the back of the tent to windward, the doors in the lee.

Once the tent was up, we turned to reinforcing it. I carved out blocks of snow, then began piling up the blocks at the south end of the tent to protect us against the wind. When I was finished, my wind wall stood three feet high and eight feet long.

Soon, snow-block walls protected the ends of all six sleeping tents. We built another wall on the windward side of the mess tent.

The wind was now so high that snow was flying horizontally across my line of sight. Alejo's Chilean flag was straight out, cracking like a cannon.

Never had I skied in a wind this strong.

I was growing increasingly worried about our resupply plane. Conditions for landing seemed impossible.

"Henry's supposed to come in tonight," Martyn had said. "We'll set up cairns on the runway so he can see where to land. He's *got* to come in."

To me, it looked impossible.

By 6:00 p.m., the tents and snow-block walls had created a funnel, building up mounds of snow four feet high and 15 feet long.

The snow in the drifts was now becoming extremely hard.

We assembled in the mess tent for dinner, but it wasn't much.

We were only a third of the way to the pole, and suffering through a blizzard outside our small camp. Low on food, even lower on fuel, we were in a potentially hazardous situation. The prospect of resupply seemed dimmer by the hour.

The mood was quiet, devoid of even the usual banter.

We were worn down, beaten by the wind, the snow, and the fatigue of skiing against the blast.

After dinner, such as it was, I stumbled back to my tent to sleep. I zipped open the flap in the freezing wind. The mess tent, though a half dozen yards away, was barely visible.

My fingers pained from the wind and flying snow. Inside, I unzipped the bag, pulled off my boots, parka, and suit and crawled in. Within minutes, I was fast asleep, dreaming of another world.

I didn't wake up until I heard a roar outside. Slowly, my mind came alive. I could not believe what I was thinking.

That noise *definitely* was the sound of engines cutting though the noise of the wind.

"We need help," Jerry yelled. *"The plane's come in."*

After jamming on my gear, I hastily crawled out of the tent into the storm.

I could hardly believe it.

The windspeed was 50 to 60 knots and the snow raced before me, biting my cheeks with a sting.

But there was the Twin Otter.

It was only 40 feet away. I could barely make out the outline; I could see that the nose of the plane was pointed directly into the wind, the door was open, and Henry was climbing out.

In a moment, Gordon Wiltsie, the *National Geographic* photographer who had come to take pictures, stepped down. I struggled around the high drifts, pushing my way to the plane.

"You made it this far," Gordon shouted encouragingly above the wind.

"What?" I yelled back. I could barely hear.

"You're going to *make it*," Gordon said. "The bets back at base camp were that you'd never do it. But if you can move in this wind, you can move in *anything*," he continued.

"We were all surprised," he added, "that you'd make it this far. The bets were you'd not get to the pole. Now I'm *sure you will.*"

As Gordon headed for the mess tent, Tori began hauling plastic food bags from the plane, and so I pitched in to help her. Everyone joined the brigade of hauling the needed supplies back to the mess tent.

In the space emptied in the plane, we loaded our garbage bags which we had carefully saved—bags filled with discarded containers.

Martyn had asked us to prepare to load any unneeded equipment—anything not absolutely essential. I shipped out my heavy Asolo boots, planning to rely instead on my much lighter Merrills. Out also went my down vest, extra pairs of underwear, socks, and my mitts.

Though Martyn said nothing, his expression revealed a deep sense of relief. My past fears of not being able to continue, of never again seeing the Twin Otter, disappeared.

The plane had brought more than supplies. It had brought *hope*.

Henry pulled out a box of brownies Lise had made for the occasion. We each got a piece.

The pilot did not tarry long. He planned to make a second drop in the Thiels—supplies which we would pick up later. The weather was so bad that Martyn decided not to join him.

Instead, he and Henry plotted on the map exactly where the depot would be placed. I watched them carefully scrutinize the large map in the mess tent.

The sun was now in the south. It was near midnight by our clocks.

We all went out into the blizzard for the takeoff. Henry climbed into the cockpit and Gordon took the co-pilot's seat.

Our hands rose in the air, waving the two goodbye. I hoped they would be able to land and to leave the cache of fuel and food that we would need.

I also hoped we could *find* the location.

With a great roar, the plane lifted off in the wind, circled once, and then turned south.

From my deep sleep sometime later, I heard a roar. I turned over happily, for I knew at once what it was: the Twin Otter had buzzed our camp after returning from the Thiels.

It meant they had succeeded.

The sound of the plane trailed off as it headed north toward the Patriot Hills and base camp. Our resupply cache lay ahead of us and was safe.

9 / CHRISTMAS

THE HOLIDAY SEASON was fast approaching, but the problems of day-to-day life on the trail held off thoughts of Christmas. I also found a new problem I had not anticipated—one that did not initially occur to me, because other problems were more pressing.

Wind, cold, constant physical exertion, and navigation problems had taken up their share of my attention. My physical ailments were no longer troubling me. My infected toe was healed, as was the sore on my crotch.

But I found that as these problems became resolved and accepted, I had a distinct new problem: my mind began to wander.

On other expeditions, I had known mental anguish, loneliness, and long hours in which my mind moved uncontrolled from one thing to another—a mind out of control.

Each morning, I started the day by reviewing the events of the previous day. After a time, these thoughts were so similar to each other they merged into one another like the white snow of one hour became that of the next.

At first, negotiating each strip of snow or finding a way over the next icy wave, consumed all my thoughts. In time, I learned to navigate the unruly snow without thought.

The actions became automatic. Much of the time, my feet would find the right way to slide without my consciously thinking about it.

It was then that I started to have mental torments.

I began to have wild imaginations. Random thoughts would emerge, expand and consume my consciousness, despite all my efforts to drive them away.

Like the sailor in mid-ocean, I worried about the turn of events at home, possibly out of guilt for being here, but mainly because there was simply nothing else to distract my attention and occupy my mind.

I began to build up deep furies which I was completely unable to control.

The uncontrolled thoughts occurred not so much because of our location here in the middle of a frozen white desert, but more from the long periods we spent in solitude. We skied six, seven, or eight hours a day.

The first hour or two were not difficult. From the start, warming up and getting used to the new day took an hour or so. Our little sleds followed patiently behind us.

Each day I again had to adjust to the wind, try to keep my goggles clear so I could see the skier ahead and the track below, watch for drops in the sastrugi. Getting into the routine of moving one foot and then the other consumed my thoughts at first.

But after a time, my thoughts would wander aimlessly. Sometimes, I tried to concentrate on past events in my life, anything to keep my mind from ceaselessly wandering at random or jealous thoughts of home.

I reviewed all the driving trips Diana and I had taken across the United States twenty years ago—east, west, south, and north.

By reviewing the trips again and again, I was able gradually to remember the roads, the cities, the hotels, memories of things I had not recalled for years.

But then I would run out of memories, or I would tire of the repetition. My mind would flow again with uncontrollable thoughts.

I felt I was like a prisoner who had no books, no paper, no one to talk to, no pen or paper, and whose mind was active and out of control.

While I had always thought I could sustain isolation without difficulty, I began to doubt myself. I found that I could no longer control my own thought processes.

The others coped with this isolation in various ways.

Shirley and Tori listened to their audio tapes. Jerry recited poetry to himself—stanzas he had memorized years ago when he had been hospitalized by injury.

Ron tuned out, an art he learned in running triathlons. Shirley made up poetry that she would recite later at dinner.

But try as I did, I was unable to recall poems or tune out my mind.

Day after day, I prayed that I might tune out completely, make my mind a blank and not wake up until I had reached the pole.

My wish was not to be fulfilled.

The best break from the mindless monotony was conversation.

Whenever I could, I latched on to someone else to talk to pass the time.

It might be discussing history or college with Tori, listening to Ron's tales of running triathlons or his various stations in the military, hearing about Shirley's past life, her days in Hawaii, or finding out about India from J.K. I listened to Jim's adventures as a mountain guide and Martyn's tales of teaching school to Indians in the Yukon.

I generally spent the last hour of each day listening to Martyn's stories or telling him some of my own. Talking with Martyn was a special treat for me, since by the last hour, I was usually near the point of exhaustion and worn out, with my legs in pain.

The conversation was like a sedative which made the hour pass quickly.

It was not the last hour that was the most difficult, but the middle of the day. The mind is a strange instrument, quite uncontrollable.

I began to sing to myself.

In an hour, I would go through each of the eight or nine songs I could remember, such as *"Oh, Susanna,"* or *"Home on the Range."*

If others were far away, I sang to my heart's content. But if they were close, I sang more quietly so as not to be overheard. For two weeks, these songs relieved an hour or two each day.

But in the end, it was the isolation, the lack of variation, the power of emptiness, the absence of anything but snow, ice, and occasional mountains, that plagued my mind and made it meander as it did.

As the weeks went by, it became not the physical effort and strain that made me wonder whether I could complete the journey, but whether I could endure those daily bouts of mental anguish.

I missed the distractions of civilized life, of the living world. I was not certain whether I would be able to go on without them.

I was barely asleep that evening when I heard voices. The sounds came filtering out of the white walls of the mess tent across the silent snow and now penetrated the nylon fabric of my tent.

"This is Walter Crankshaft," the voice seemed to say. *"Walter Crankshaft."*

Static interrupted the voice. There was something odd going on here.

Was it the radio? I wondered. *Could I be dreaming?*

"Good morning," the radio voice said. "The weather in Patriot Hills is clear. There is a light wind."

At first I could not imagine what I was hearing. Then, the reality slowly sank in.

"Conditions at base camp are excellent," the voice continued.

"We have a report from the South Pole Overland Expedition. They are continuing their effort to reach the South Pole. *Can you believe it?"*

"The latest report states that Jerry Corr has involved fellow expedition member and tent-mate Joseph Murphy in a business swindle. Murphy reportedly has been fleeced of $1 million in a real estate scam. Corr stole the money."

Crankshaft, Crankshaft, I puzzled. That sounds like a takeoff on Cronkite, *Walter Cronkite.*

The radio crackled slightly as I tried to identify the circumstances and voice.

The mock-serious report continued: "Murphy, it is said, is furious with Corr for the swindle and in retaliation has moved out of their tent. He now sleeps on the frozen ice in his bivouac sack."

I began to chuckle.

There was a pause.

Then an advertisement for South Pole Pancakes, the specialty of Martyn Williams, renowned chef.

"We have a second report from Punta Arenas," the voice continued. I wondered who was talking. It sounded a little like Gordon.

"It is said that Colin Campbell has taken off from Punta Arenas with Martyn Williams' DC-4 and is headed for Argentina. Dissatisfied with his meager wages, Colin plans to sell the plane in Argentina. This means, of course, that the expedition members will have no means of returning from Antarctica."

I laughed at the report. It was Gordon Wiltsie, the Geographic photographer. He sounded authentic—and had a good knack for mimicking what television reporters say.

The next night, Gordon came on again. And the night after that. He continued to broadcast nightly for some time to the entire Antarctica continent. I was certain he could be heard from as far south as the pole and as far north as Punta Arenas.

I wondered what the rest of the Antarctic world thought about our comic broadcasts. If they did hear and think about them, I never heard.

The frozen continent was completely silent on its reaction.

The days had slipped by imperceptibly. I had left Minnesota on Thanksgiving day. I had known I would be gone for Christmas, but the thought of spending Christmas in Antarctica did not really sink in until that day began to draw quite near.

I had always approached Christmas with mixed feelings, particularly as I got older. The prospect of too many presents was more pain than pleasure, especially when I received things I could not use.

Partly because of this view, one of my favorite Christmases had been spent abroad where there were few presents. We had gone to Lech, Austria, with my cousin's family. Elaborate preparations were eliminated and Christmas became a simple affair—few presents, good skiing, little ceremony.

Consequently, I almost looked with relief to Christmas in Antarctica, where there could not possibly be any presents. With our weight-conscious loads, we had nothing to give.

At the same time, it had not occurred to me that we would not take Christmas day off. Nearly a half-century of Christmas holidays had ingrained in me that Christmas was a day of rest. Christmas day, from my earliest memory, was to be free to do as one wished.

Of course, I understood our present need to keep pushing for the pole, to use every day that was clear to move on. Yet, I was completely unprepared when at the end of breakfast on December 25, Martyn announced: "We'll start at nine. Okay, everyone?"

This silenced any thoughts I had of a long-due holiday. There would be no relaxation in the pace, no taking time off. During the day, at least, Christmas would not be celebrated.

Jerry and I dropped the tent, according to our custom, rolled it up, and then I hauled the tent and my duffel to the main sledge so they could be loaded up before our continuation south.

Christmas day was clear. A light wind played over us. The sun lay in the east, its normal place at this time of day. It would circle around—another rotation for another day. The snow beneath our skis glistened in the sun.

I jammed my Merrill ski boots into the front of my bindings, pushed the latch down with my cold fingers, picked up the line to my red sled, and made ready to start.

Tori took the lead for the first hour, as she did every morning and we started off. I tried to get up front near Tori so I would have less difficulty keeping up. Thus the day was like any other, nothing special.

We alternated leads after Tori's initial start. We attempted to keep in line, as hard as the rough waves of snow made that attempt.

My thoughts wandered. Most of the time, I thought about matters other than Christmas, the cold after the break, the interminable fog of my lenses, the perspiration that accumulated once I warmed up. I watched the cloud formations come and go.

I imagined my wife, Diana, and our sons, Michael and John, snuggled in our cabin in northern Minnesota on the shore of Lake Superior. They had promised to go there over Christmas, as we had each year since acquiring the log cabin.

Then my memory lapsed into the continuing drudgery of the push toward the pole.

The snowmobiles arrived early at our next campsite, their sledges trailing behind. Mike lined up his sledge on the left, looking south. Stewart took the right side. Between the two sledges, we erected the mess tent and hauled in supplies.

By the time I finished putting up my sleeping tent, I had pretty much forgotten about the holiday.

But when I returned to the mess tent, Martyn was ready.

To my surprise, there was a Christmas feast: hot turkey, real dressing, corn, cauliflower, potatoes, cowboy coffee, and pie.

It brought tears to my eyes and memories of Christmases past.

The Christmas feast at the South Pole was on.

Even J.K., who was not Christian but Hindu, relished the event as much as anyone.

After dinner, in high spirits, Stewart disappeared out the east door.

When he returned, he was dressed in a bunny suit. Somehow, he had put it on over his cold-weather gear.

With evident pleasure, he began distributing presents. He had a present for each of us with our name inscribed on the package. The package contained whistles, streamers, fake noses, chocolate candy, gumdrops, and assorted other delicacies.

Our holiday celebration continued as Ron and Shirley took over to mastermind the "lack of talent show." Ron acted an imitation of Johnny Carson and Shirley acted like Barbara Walters.

I saw a talent in Ron I had not noticed before as he did a fair imitation of Johnny Carson introducing his guests, which just happened to be the other 10 of us, complete with impertinent descriptions of our individual talents.

We each were expected to put on an act. To me, this was like days in school when you were expected to get up and perform, though you would much prefer to stay hidden at the back of the room. Not everyone was reluctant, I discovered—certainly not Stuart or Shirley.

Real talent did appear, unexpectedly, in the form of a song composed by Mike, the refrain of which was:

South Pole, South Pole, it's a long way to go.
It's all green, but it's covered with snow.
If you think that to go so far is completely absurd.
You should come visit us at home in our TURD.

By the end of the show, most of us had tears in our eyes, not simply because it was Christmas, but because we were celebrating together, because we had come so far and because we had begun to suspect that we now had a fair chance of actually reaching the South Pole.

As a result of our long, mutual effort, a bond was forming among us, a bond that would last for a long time, a bond that became evident in this Christmas ceremony which I had hoped might not take place.

I was glad that it had.

10 / ACROSS THE
CREVASSE FIELD

THE DAY AFTER CHRISTMAS was a significant
milestone: it was the day we passed the halfway mark,
the day we crossed into 85-degree latitude. That meant
we had but five degrees left.

We had also passed more than the halfway point in
miles. By the end of the day, we would have completed
383 miles.

Reaching this milestone brought on speculation. We
had begun to count miles: how much of the route had
been done, how much was left to be done.

And we counted days—all guessing at the expected
date of arrival. Jim and Martyn bet daily on this
speculation. I made daily mental calculations on our
progress and on how far we had left to go.

It was comforting to make these countdowns. It was

now the first day of the fifth week. I kept myself going partly by remembering the original estimate of 45 days: six weeks, and three days. I knew it would take longer than that to get to the pole, but by the time six weeks were done, we'd be very close.

To plot our route, we relied on a topographic map of the Thiel Mountains, with a scale of 1:50,000. The map, prepared by the U.S. Geological Survey, was detailed, showing the range itself, the peaks, the blue ice, and the crevasses.

The only difficulty lay in the contour lines, which were 200 meters apart (roughly 600 feet), and not at all enough to determine how much altitude we gained or lost or to compare the relative difficulty of various routes. Moreover, the Thiel range did not run due north and south but at 15 degrees variance to due south.

To reach the polar plateau, we had to cross the Thiels. The range itself formed a barrier between our position and the South Pole. We could not cross them directly, since the granite peaks towered 3,000 feet above the flat ice and snow.

From examining the topographic map, I observed that we had two choices for crossing this barrier. The first was to ski west around the western end; the second was to parallel the range to the eastern end.

If we went around the western edge, we would ski over barren wasteland and have to climb. We decided to go east.

All day on December 27, we ran along the Thiels but at a great distance from the mountains. The direction of our route was clear, for the mountains guided our steps. Once again, the wind was high, 25 miles per hour, gusting to 40, and the day was cold. Pushing against that wind and in the cold sapped our energy, and we could not have made it without our protective Scott masks.

The Thiel Mountains contained our cache, which had been set up earlier by Henry and his air drop. This was the resupply of food, fuel, and stove gas that we needed before Henry was again destined to visit our camp, many days away.

Originally, we had decided to ski as a group to the cache, but now, with the decision to cross the mountain range on the left, the cache was 10 miles out of the way. We skiers went on ahead, and the snowmobiles made the run to the cache, picking up the 21 day's worth of food and fuel. Then they backtracked and, toward the end of the day, joined us.

We were all tired by camp, but we had made good time, even with the wind and cold. By the time I had finally crawled into my sleeping bag, my toes felt frozen; it took a long time for them to warm up.

One pair of liner socks against the intense cold, I told myself, is not enough. I need more.

Today, we hoped to cross the barrier of the Thiel Mountains. We planned to climb the ramp of snow just north of King Peak, but from our camp, we could not tell whether the route was crevassed or could be climbed by either skiers or snowmobiles. If it was not passable, we would have to round the Thiel range at its most southern extremity, far out of our way.

It was another cold, windy day. The catabatic gusts funneled down the ramp we wished to ascend and hit the snowfield we were crossing with force. As the day progressed, we could see the blue ice that formed the basement of every range. It was a very large expanse, hard and blue, and reminded me of a glacier lake bordering the foot of a mountain.

When we finally reached the ice, we skirted left to avoid crossing the main part. To reach the snow ramp leading to the plateau above, we had to cross the last section of ice. There, to my surprise, I found that the force of the wind had lessened. The ice was marked by thin lines of snow, like the stray threads left by a spider, barely visible but potentially treacherous.

But now I saw snow hid crevasses, a few inches to a foot wide—and of unknown depth.

I had removed my skis to avoid slipping and cracking my head on the smooth surface when Martyn warned:

"Watch your step, or you'll go through the *crevasse* below."

Not really certain that the snow-filled cracks were deep or that the snow was not hard, we edged our way along the snow so we would not chance slipping on the ice. Jerry was ahead of me, Martin behind.

I had my skis over my shoulder, the tips balanced under one arm. I dragged my sled behind, tied to my waist by a rope.

My memory flooded with past escapes from crevasses. I had been lucky: I had never fallen in—not far, anyway. Not deeper than my waist.

I remembered the story of a climber on Mount McKinley, who had fallen head-first into a crevasse. He had been lodged so tightly between the walls, and had fallen so far, that his climbing partner was unable to rescue him and had to leave him to perish in that unnatural deep-freeze position. The memory of this story had come back every time I crossed a crevasse field.

The memory came back now.

We were moving with caution, especially since, in order to save weight, we had left behind most of our Jumars, slings and ropes—our crevasse rescue equipment. Should someone fall into a crevasse now, we could be in a great deal of trouble.

The snow in the crack seemed quite firm, and I

continued along it, daring my fate, when someone cried, *"Jerry's gone through!"*

"What happened?"

"Jerry fell in a *crevasse*," Shirley yelled back.

I looked about and could not see him.

Then, I saw: Jerry's legs had disappeared. Only his upper body was visible. He had thrust his hands and arms out and stopped his fall.

To our amazement, just as quickly as he had fallen in, Jerry extricated himself.

"He's *all right*," Tori said with relief.

What had happened was that, moving like the rest of us, Jerry had stepped through the fragile snow that covered the deep cracks in the ice and had gone through to his waist.

But he had caught himself. Fortunately the crack was narrow and he did not fall far.

But it was a scare—after that we all moved more carefully.

"Stay off the snow," Martin warned.

We proceeded on to the far side of the blue ice. Above was a smooth slope, also marked by similar lines that concealed equally dangerous crevasses. The top of the slope was 600 feet above us.

"Go single file," warned Martyn. "That way, only one of us will go through, not everyone."

We started up the slope. Jerry would be the unlucky one again, for he had taken the lead. We continued, in single file, making jokes about the crevasse danger. But no one went in, not even Jerry.

At the top of the slope, the wind died and that night, we were able to camp well beyond the Thiels, though still within view of the range. We had gotten through—and we had been lucky. We would not realize exactly how lucky we had been until much later.

11 / WHITEOUT

AT 7:00 IN THE MORNING, Jerry was jubilant. "Clear weather," he shouted when he crawled out of the tent. His joy was short-lived, for by the time we left camp, we were encircled by clouds. Visibility dropped quickly, from 500 feet to less than 100. *Whiteout.*

We struggled blind, but for our compasses. We snaked across the vast plain like pilgrims on a journey toward a goal whose location was not quite known. We were headed for the last nunatak, the last beacon on our route to the pole.

Beyond that, there would be nothing to guide us on the flat, wide, featureless plain that stretched 300 miles to the pole.

The whiteout was distressing to all of us, especially to the lead person. We plodded on through the windless whiteness, slowly, step by step.

My skis kept sliding off the slopeing, which cut diagonally across our route. When the snow became hard and unbreakable, I switched to walking. The holes in the sastrugi were deep, often two feet or more, and I could not see where to put my skis or my feet. It was like walking in a cloud full of hidden traps.

Though we erected snow cairns at frequent intervals, finding us was going to be extremely difficult for the Ski-Doos. Martyn became worried that the machines could not find our tracks and called a halt to further movement.

In the heavy mist, we set up the two tents we carried on our sleds for emergency and crawled inside. Tori placed ski poles every 20 feet perpendicular to our line of movement so that the Ski-Doos could find them if they missed the cairns.

Jim, J.K., Alejo, and I crawled in one tent, the rest in the other. I did not have my seat pad, so Alejo, who had carried two, lent me one to sit on. While we waited for Mike and Stuart to arrive, we told climbing stories. Though the heat of our bodies gradually warmed the tent, my toes began to freeze as minutes turned into hours. There was no sun to warm our shelter this day.

Martyn made periodic calls on his radio: "Ski-Doo, Ski-Doo, Ski-Doo. This is skiers, skiers, skiers. Over."

There was no response. We had no communication with the Ski-Doos. The machines were probably below a rise, no longer in line of sight for our high-frequency radios. For a long time we wondered what had happened.

Suddenly, the oppressing silence was disturbed by a distant rumble. The machines were coming in.

They had found our way.

Travel had been difficult for the Ski-Doos in the rough sastrugi and poor visibility. The drivers could not see the deep dropoffs until they were nearly over them. Only the tracks of our boots in the hard snow enabled them to follow our route. The cairns were too far apart.

One sledge had overturned, and the gasoline had spilled out on part of the load, forcing the drivers to reload. This had delayed their arrival at our temporary camp.

When the machines roared up, we quickly struck the tents, gathered up the ski poles Tori had set out, and resumed our march. The sky cleared just enough to enable partial vision of the nunatak ahead.

But underneath, the surface remained hidden, making our footing perilous.

J.K. took a painful fall into a four-foot hole. For the rest of the day, he followed my example and walked, but the rest stuck resolutely to their skis.

In the whiteout, we walkers were able to keep pace with the skiers, even to pass them.

My hope of crossing 86 degrees latitude by year end were dashed. The day was cloudy, visibility extremely low, and the temperature hovered around zero with only a slight wind.

Skiing in the clouds with heavy sastrugi had been harrowing.

Because of the poor visibility, we had a discussion at breakfast the next day on the advisability of taking a rest day.

Shirley said that she absolutely needed a day off. J.K. gave an extended lecture on the importance of rest. "We have been on the trail for 32 days," he emphasized, "with only three days of rest."

"That's one day in ten—absolutely not enough."

In our tired, tense state, a fall and a broken leg could

happen to any of us. If one of us broke a leg, we might be set back a week. It was best to avoid that possibility.

Jerry, Ron, and I all voted to move on. Tori agreed, as well, until she heard Shirley's insistence. We decided to halt for the day. That turned out to be a fortunate decision in view of the rough tracking that was to come.

When I got outside, I noticed that ski poles had been set out in various directions. "Find the compass reading to that pole," Martyn said.

I reset my magnetic declination to the proper reading and then took a sight on the pole Martyn had pointed out. I knew Martyn was concerned about our ability to travel correctly, particularly if the poor visibility continued. We each took bearings, marched off toward the poles, took new bearings on the return, and practiced setting a course of direction and following it. Martyn and Jim checked our results on each bearing.

The visibility improved slightly during the afternoon, and Shirley took videos of the camp and our activities. Part of the group set off to climb Lewis Nunatak, including Stuart, Alejo, Tori, Mike, and Ron, who returned refreshed.

The rest of us slept, wrote letters, worked on diaries, or read.

Our physical condition varied. Tori's left wrist was out of joint, and she had to wear a brace. Both Jerry and Shirley had three-inch blisters on their heels, which forced each of them to wear extra-large boots with a large pad to protect the blister. Jim, who had done the medical work, was afraid to break their blisters for fear of causing blood poisoning. Martyn was still recovering from injuries from his fall, and he had contracted a sore throat. The rest of us were in good condition.

Martyn had became even more concerned about our navigation and wanted to increase the number of sun readings. To facilitate taking readings, he wanted to reset our watches by four hours so that sightings could be taken during the day. For each sighting, the sun would be in the right position.

The following morning, Shirley took her video camera to record the last scenes with any visible features, the Lewis Nunatak, which lay a short distance south of camp. She wanted to be certain to get pictures while she had the chance.

The wind was light and a half-inch of snow lay over the sastrugi. This was the best skiing we'd had so far. Alejo raced ahead, up the slope, far to our left, while the rest of us stayed in line. The morning sun cast shadows to our left. To the right, a mile away, lay a long ridge paralleling our route, white, with only an occasional outcrop of rock. It was the eastern flank of the plateau that ran south of the western part of the Thiel Mountains.

The first hour on the trail was deceptive, for the soft snow quickly turned into deep drifts of hard sastrugi. When Alejo took the lead, he moved forward, never looking down but straight on, crossing directly over every obstacle, sometimes waves of snow that were 5 and 10 feet tall. I was sure he was going to break his neck.

I gave him the nickname "Directo Alejo," which seemed to amuse him.

The snow was so hard and chaotic that I again switched to walking, hoisting my skis over my shoulder and carrying them.

"Can I take your skis on my sled?" Alejo kept asking.

"No, but thanks," I replied. The light skis were no burden, and I could switch them from one shoulder to another to relieve any soreness. The others stuck to their skis, and later on, when the snow became soft I switched back to skis.

We skied so close in line that it was sometimes hard to keep from tripping over one another. This was actually ironic in a place as vast as this, where the population density measured thousands of square miles per person.

Suddenly, my ski caught Tori's ski, and down she went in a bad fall.

"I'm sorry," I said.

"It's nothing," she replied.

But I could see that it was not nothing. Tori took off her skis and walked the rest of the day. She had further damaged her wrist.

It was badly out of joint. But she made no complaint.

We continued our hard march over the rough-and-tumbled snow.

"Ski-Doos," someone shouted.

We saw Mike and Stuart on two Ski-Doos with two sledges—but only one load.

"The blade twisted under," Mike said. "We had to leave the load. We'll get it later."

The corrugated terrain had been too much. One sledge was ruptured and had to be repaired before it could carry a load. The loads had been rearranged, the unneeded equipment and supplies left behind, and the essentials brought forward.

We set up camp as usual, and after a time, Stuart returned with the good sledge to pick up the abandoned gear.

It was New Year's Eve, time to celebrate. For the occasion, Martyn made Irish stew and provided red and white wine in cardboard cartons.

Stuart, again wearing his bunny suit, distributed another round of presents.

Though we stayed up past midnight, we offset the

lateness by setting our watches back two hours to begin adapting to the new time schedule.

Today, on the first day of the new year, the outlook was good. At about two degrees below zero, it was slightly warmer than yesterday, and the sky was clear and sunny. Long layers of clouds lay far to the west.

The wind was light, and the sastrugi were small. A soft snow, perhaps a half-inch deep, covered the hard surface so that skiing was easy. It was like cross-country skiing at home, over a flat surface, a good track that the skis could make and we could follow. It was a wonderful day, as our thin, long skis moved smoothly over the flat surface on a visible trail.

In a group so small, on an expedition so long, personality conflict often occurs. Despite occasional altercations and disagreements, we got on fairly well. This was important, for any one of us could jeopardize the entire expedition in any number of ways: simply by refusing to go forward, by rejecting the leadership of Martyn, or by feigning illness or injury.

But no one had reneged or complained about the constant grind. It was a remarkable display of cooperation and determination for a group so disparate and so randomly joined together in this unusual enterprise.

Of all members of the expedition, the one that puzzled me most was Shirley. She exhibited the most energy, the most intensity, and the most outward ambition. I noticed in the mess tent that, when the rest of us were making sandwiches or telling stories or bantering one another with good humor, Shirley was hard at work on one project or another: writing in her diary, reading her poems, preparing dispatches to be sent out to NBC, taking movies, putting on skin cream, or sewing. She seemed driven to activity to a degree the rest of us were not.

This was even characteristic of Shirley's pulse rate, which, instead of declining as it should as the weeks went by, kept climbing, ultimately exceeding 90.

Jim said to me one day, "I thought she might crack."

"I never doubted that I would make the pole," Shirley told me on several occasions, though she admitted that the first two weeks had been a "matter of survival."

Scott's entire party had died within a short distance of their last food cache.

Shackleton had not made it. Shirley seemed oblivious to the things that could cause failure.

And they were many.

12 / AIR RESUPPLY

Every day, I counted the miles made, the miles to go, the degrees covered, and the degrees remaining. I hoped that doing so would somehow reduce the drudgery and relieve the intense loneliness of the journey.

I had the pervasive desire to be done, to be home once again. There were moments of joy: times when I looked at the roof of the sky, marveled at the long streams of clouds that ran to infinity, or treasured the beauty of the varying forms of snow underfoot.

But these times of relishing the glory of this barren wilderness were passing moments only. Between them were the long hours of grinding on.

Today, I was comforted by the easy skiing and the low 10-mile-per-hour wind. We skied 19 miles and crossed the 86th parallel. We had covered nearly two-thirds of the total distance, and we had but four degrees to go.

We were now putting one degree behind us every four days.

Progress indeed. Our prospects for making the pole were excellent—if we could keep up this remarkable pace.

Our relief from the constant push forward was talk. We reminisced about the trip, speculated on when we might reach the pole, told tales of relatives or friends, and listened to one another's concerns.

But talk wasn't always possible; usually it was not. The pace might be too fast, the snow too rough, or the visibility too poor. But still the need for talk was always there. Tori put the matter succinctly one morning when she said, "Talk to me, Joe, or I'll go mad."

Today was a good time to talk. The cloudy sky had turned to a clear brilliant blue. Skiing conditions were perfect; there was an inch of powder over mild forms of snow.

When I spotted Shirley coming up behind me, struggling with the video equipment she had brought today, I seized the opportunity. I had not talked to her on the trail for a long time, and I desperately needed some conversation.

"How's my skiing pal?" I asked. "

I noticed that Shirley had a limp, favoring her left side, and that her left arm hung down. But when I inquired, she said she had a muscle problem and a problem with her lung. Apparently the pain arose from an injury she had suffered as a child.

When Martyn came up, he suggested that she stop carrying her entire load. J.K. had graciously offered to share Shirley's load.

So at the next break, the heavy video equipment was divided among Ron, Martyn, and J.K. But three hours later, when we customarily made our decision to go on or not to go on to 6:30, J.K. said he wanted to stop at 6:00. We had long ago agreed that, if only one person wanted to stop, we all would stop. So we halted for the day at 6:00.

We had been going at a steady pace for days, skiing 18 to 20 miles, counting the miles done, pressing on to increase the count, pushing on to the latest possible hour, to 6:30—nine hours a day. I was not conscious of the tension, but it must have been there. The constant pressure to push on and on and on must have affected everyone, perhaps only unconsciously.

It emerged unexpectedly. Jerry and I were in our tent, just after getting the mess tent up and erecting our own bare shelter. I was already in my bag, long underwear changed, trying to arrange my mitts in the net just above my head so the frozen pile would thaw by morning.

Something seemed to be going on in the nearby tent shared by the two colonels, but I could not tell what. I heard only the voices of Shirley and Martyn who were not normally next door. J.K. was upset about something.

"We'll discuss it after dinner," I heard him say.

We had our usual discussion after dinner, which Martyn initiated every evening to work out problems, to allow us to voice complaints, and to make suggestions. This was a good idea, for it usually led to improvements in our daily routine. At these meetings, we also set the time of departure, the time of halting for the day, the number of breaks, the time spent at each break, and how we skied as a group.

Martyn usually controlled the topics and limited them to the ones he wanted to discuss. He avoided other matters, such as the route we might take or the disposition of the snowmobiles. If we brought them up, he simply left the questions in abeyance, handling only those matters he wanted to.

Tonight J.K. was angry.

"There was no relationship between my taking part of Shirley's load and wanting to stop at 6 o'clock," he snapped. "The last half hour is of no importance. We usually get a late start anyway, because Joe is always late."

It was true; I peaked at 5. But I didn't like my being late brought up where I felt it had no relevance.

"You should go on at 6 without me," I said.

But J.K. had not finished. "The breaks are not seven minutes as they should be, but often 15 minutes. I timed them myself."

It was obvious J.K. did not like being criticized for calling an early halt after sharing part of Shirley's load. But the magnitude of the altercation was symptomatic of the strain that affected us all.

"You don't have to be in front, J.K.," Mike said to break the tension.

"You can stay in back," he said, with a grin, "and set the pace from there."

Even J.K. had to laugh—and that was the end of the conflict. We quickly returned to our usual evening bantering, telling stories, and kidding around. The problem had ended as quickly as wit broke the tension.

I heard someone saying, "*Joe. It's 7 o'clock. Time to get up.*"

Though I was faintly aware of my tent-mate's rummaging, his announcement was the first thing in the morning I paid attention to. At first, I obeyed the gentle instruction and began preparing for the day.

But as the weeks passed, I found I could sleep for another half hour (doze would be more accurate), and still make the start-off time of half past 9.

My routine was systematic and I kept it exactly the same every morning.

During the night, I had unzipped the sleeping bag halfway open to cool off in the heat of the sun now on my side of the tent. Now, all I had to do in the morning, was roll the bag around until the zipper was on top.

Then I sat up, took off the heavy poly underwear I'd worn during the night, and put on the second poly for the day. I switched from the heavy night underwear to light for the day and then put on the poly pants. Next, I reached for my one-piece suit. I always stretched it out along the outside of the tent to help protect me from the wind and any snow that had been piled up alongside the tent. If the suit had gotten wet from perspiration the prior day, it was dry by morning.

I pulled on the legs of the suit, hitched the rest up over my back and arms, pulled the zipper up to my neck, and if it was especially cold, I pulled the hood over my head. Once the suit was on, I reached into the clear plastic bag behind me for my heavy socks, which I pulled on immediately before my feet started to get cold. Once my feet got cold, it was very hard to warm them up.

Then I checked my pile mitt liners to see if any ice or snow remained from the day before. Generally they were perfectly dry.

I reached forward to the other end of the tent to get the mitt shells, which I had hung the night before by the door opening to allow them to dry. I inserted the pile liners inside the nylon outers, making sure the thumb was correct.

Next I checked my ski boots for any remaining ice; if there was, I scraped it out with my fingernails so my feet wouldn't get cold during the day. Next I held the boots upside down and banged them together to knock out frost. This done, I set the boots on the insulating mat to dry out further.

Last came my regular boots, heavy parka, and hat. I pulled out the heavy parka from underneath the head of the sleeping bag, where it had served as a pillow, then pushed my arms in, pulled it up and yanked the zipper. Usually, the zipper caught, and I had to spend several minutes freeing it. Then I put on my pile hat and pulled the fur-lined hood of the parka up over my head.

By this time, I would begin to get cold. Within a few seconds, the parka warmed me up again. I pulled on the heavy white boots, tied the laces, and was ready once again to face the polar cold.

I grabbed my pee bottle to empty it outside, unzipped the three zippers on the doors of the tent, and crawled out. No one was in the latrine. I walked slowly over in the bright light and wind to make the same morning call I had made every day for the past five weeks.

Cirrus clouds covered the sky very high up, and a light wind played upon the hard sastrugi. We set off on time and kept to J.K.'s recommendation of seven-minute breaks. The hard waves of snow in the first hour soon gave way to soft snow, making the skiing easy.

To pass the time, I skied alone and sang all the songs I could remember, from *"Old Man River"* to *"Oh, Susanna,"* bellowing out the words when I thought no one could hear. With the singing, the day passed quickly.

We put in our *best distance* to date: *22 miles.* "At this rate, we can do a degree in three days," I said to Martyn.

By the end of the day, we had passed the 500-mile mark and had but 250 miles to go. "We are two-thirds of the way," I said to Jerry, as I clapped him on the back. "Only *one-third* to go."

Jerry beamed. He was as ecstatic as I.

Our schedule was now nearly automatic. Jerry was

always up first. After emerging from the tent, he woke up whoever was to make breakfast—Martyn, Jim, Stuart, or Alejo. Then he went into the mess tent to get hot cocoa or coffee. He and Shirley cut the cheese and salami for lunch and laid out the luncheon foods—bread, dried fruit and chocolate bars—a task they completed nearly every day. Then Shirley finished with her makeup, using the kit she had brought with her.

Seven-thirty was the breakfast call. I usually arrived by 7:45. Alejo was always last, Jim next to the last, while Tori and Ron arrived somewhere in between. The breakfast menu alternated eggs, oatmeal, or pancakes. By 8:30 most of us were out to our own tents to pack our sleeping bags, tape blistered feet, stuff our duffel bags, and take down our tents. We waxed our skis in the last few minutes before 9:30, the scheduled starting time. Packing the sledges and taking down the mess tent were left to Mike and Stuart.

Today was no exception. We left right on schedule. Tori led for an hour and a half to the first break at 11 and then Ron took over. The day was clear, the temperature a few degrees above zero, and the wind 15 to 20 miles per hour, slightly lower in the afternoon. By midday, the soft snow changed to hard sastrugi two to three feet deep.

Danger comes quickly in the Antarctic. Sometimes, you don't even know what can harm you until too late.

Unknown to us, we had skied over a broad field of crevasses two to three miles long.

Had we been walking, or the snow been less hard, any of us might have disappeared.

We didn't learn about it until the Twin Otter pilot, looking for cairns that marked our way, spotted the danger and later told us about it.

He and his co-pilot had been very worried.

As the week wore on, the cold seemed to change. The intense cold that at first was so deeply penetrating gradually seemed to lessen a little.

It was not that I was always in shivers, but I was continuously aware of the cold, *every* hour and *every* day. I was even cold at the end of our hourly break, when the excess heat thrown off by constant work disappeared as we sat on our packs.

I often sat with my back to the wind, looking out at the blank white snow beyond. Like horses standing huddled against the wind, we huddled, close to the ground. I looked at my legs stretched out, resting, my arms held close to my body to conserve heat, my mitts and even my frozen mask always in place.

Quickly, I'd slip my hand out of the mitt, grasp something to munch on from my pack, or take a needed swig from the warm canteen. But even this simple act was fraught with threat: if I kept my hand out too long, or exposed it unnecessarily in the wind that rarely ceased, it would begin to lose all sensation. The extremities of the fingers would become numb and even my thick thumbs would get cold.

If I were lucky, my hand eventually would warm up. But I knew it would not thaw out right away, for on every start my fingers were usually frozen. The wet liner mitts drew off the perspiration and cooled down the fingers rapidly.

Never, not once, it seemed, did my fingers warm up for the first 15 minutes on the trail. They remained slightly stiff, pained with cold.

But on those stops when I tarried too long, it might take a full hour of skiing to revive them. Cold. Cold. Cold fingers, cold body.

It was less painful for me than for some of the others, especially Jerry.

"Let's go," he would call. *"Let's go!"*

Then, with a jerk, he would be off: skiing rapidly, shoving his legs behind him, doing everything to revive the warmth of his body, to heat up his limbs.

Compared to Jerry, I was warm-blooded. Jerry was always cold, cold at the break, cold in the tent, cold at the end of the day. I was often cold, but Jerry was colder. Yet he never complained.

As the weeks wore on, the mean temperature dropped. It had been 18 degrees above at the start of the edge of the Ronne Ice Shelf, at 80 degrees south latitude. It was now chilling down to 18 degrees below zero as we neared the pole.

But the thermometer reading did not take into account the wind chill. When the wind hit 30 knots, the wind chill dropped sharply to -50 and even to -80.

With my face in the wind, I confronted immediate freezing.

But Shirley had provided us with large plastic face shields. I recalled how I had first fitted the black face mask on, pulled over my goggles, then examined the results in the mirror. Staring back at me was Darth Vader from *Star Wars*.

Now, my face was covered: not an inch of pink was revealed.

That was fortunate. Today, the wind speed was 32 knots and straight in our faces. The masks deflected the full force and kept us from freezing.

One day, far into the trip, the wind shifted sharply, angling from the south-southeast. It was just far enough to one side to slip between my plastic face mask and hat.

By the afternoon, I noticed my left cheek had become hard and unfeeling.

"Your face is frozen," Mike Sharp said that night. "You better tape it, or you'll lose the skin."

"One freezing is no problem," I said. "But two are."

I taped the skin, but as the next few days wore on, I wondered if the frostbitten area would heal or if I would lose some skin permanently. I kept the tape on just in case.

Tori also had suffered frostbite on her right cheek. She had covered part of her face with bandages.

Each day, Alejo took our altitude with his altimeter. We started this day at 7,710 feet and ended at 8,130, a rise of 420 feet. Yesterday, we had gained 400 feet and the day before 420 feet. In 12 of the last 14 days, we were higher at the end of the day than we were at the beginning.

This gradual, but nearly steady rise in elevation was not at all what I had expected. We had been told that, beyond the Thiels, we would attain the "Polar Plateau." But there was no plateau, only a slowly rising plain. Since the pole itself was at 9,300 feet, we still had 1,600 feet to climb.

Between Patriot Hills and the pole, a distance equal to that between New York and Chicago, the only form of life was that of the 11 skiers who were crossing the continent. There was no other life, not a wolf, bird, ant, or fly. There was not even any evidence of life. The continent was simply too dry, too cold, and too inhospitable to support any other living organism.

Though the continent resembled our great plains in winter, it was sterile like a great, clean room where no bacteria, not a single virus lived. It was so void of organisms that those humans who returned from Antarctica frequently caught contagious diseases, because their bodies had become unaccustomed to external microbes.

Unlike the lower peninsula of Antarctica, which teemed with penguins, skua, walruses and other life, we saw and encountered nothing alive. Or, so it seemed.

Then one day far into our journey, as we pushed our skis up what I felt was an unending hill, I felt the wind against my face.

The air was rushing past me at perhaps 15 or 20 knots. The sun was in the west, slanting its rays across the snow which sparkled in the yellow light.

I was immersed in thought when I heard a sound I had not heard before.

It was not a human sound, not the noise of the snowmobiles, not the Twin Otter which was not due for some time. It was a strange sound, a call, an unexpected utterance. Turning to the rear, I glanced around. But I saw nothing.

Then, quite suddenly, I noticed a shadow fleeting across the snow.

Looking up, I saw two small white birds vigorously flapping their wings against the wind. The creatures were behind us, flying furiously to keep us in view. They were two Arctic terns, their ivory wings reflected in the sun.

Very gradually, they approached us, beating their wings very hard to avoid being swept away by the heavy movement of the air. They seemed curious about us—as curious as we were about them.

Jerry swung his skis around so he could take a picture. When he did so, they darted away. Tori brought food over to where the birds were suspended, but once again they retreated north.

Then they returned, more interested in us than in the food. The isolated creatures were more than 400 miles from any source of food, water, or anything else to keep them alive.

The wind was so rough that the two creatures bounced about, yet they finally closed the gap between us. Soon, they were within 20 yards. Their curious stares continued as they flapped not more than six feet off the surface of the snow.

They observed us very intently. Several of us managed to get pictures. Then, the birds wheeled off to investigate the other skiers to our rear.

As I watched, I wondered what would happen to these lone creatures so far from home. Once we started off again, the birds disappeared.

I wondered if we would ever see them again.

The sastrugi were extremely rough, with one-to two-foot holes common. Some were as deep as five feet.

An hour into the run, I felt severe pain in my left leg all the way from my butt to my foot. Pain in one or both legs was common during the first couple of hours each day, but it was not usually severe, and had always disappeared by 11 o'clock or noon.

Today was quite different. The pain was so severe that I doubted I could keep going. As I tried to diagnose the cause, I recalled that I felt a sharp pain last night lifting one of the boxes. The pain had recurred during the night. Perhaps it was that.

Or, perhaps it was caused by the wedge that was put on one of my skis. Shirley had told me that the wedge might cause pain because it altered the way my body was aligned.

To relieve the pain, I switched to walking and by mid-afternoon, I had some relief. That night, over the radio, Lise prescribed muscle-relaxing pills, which I was to take for the next three days.

The immediate effect of the pills was that I slept soundly the entire night, not waking early in the morning, as usual. Just in case the wedge had caused the problem, Alejo removed it from my ski. Even with the wedge gone, I wondered whether the pain would come back tomorrow.

The cold of the day gave way to the cold of the night. It wasn't night, exactly, for the sun never went down, never sank out of sight.

But as the skiers picked their campsite at the day's end, their thoughts turned to their own shelters. When we had erected the mess tent, the "TURD," we immediately started on our own tents.

Putting up our sleeping tent was a cold affair, especially at first before I had learned how to thread the poles through the sleeves of the outer tent wall with my gloves on. The first week or so I needed to take my gloves off.

Taking them off seemed innocent enough, but it took some minutes to thread the poles through. Or, the Kevlar poles would snap away or move. More often than not, I couldn't get the front loop in. Jerry and I would struggle, curse above the howl of the wind, and finally jam them in.

All the while, the wind blasted across my fingers, which I couldn't see because my goggles had frosted up. It was a cold and miserable time, with snow flying in your face, the yellow walls of the tent flapping like the blade of a helicopter, the whole process intractable.

Then, you looked at your fingers and saw they were looking a bit white. You'd touch them to your other hand and slowly realize *there was no feeling*. They had lost all *sensation*. The knowledge of what that might mean reached your mind and you began to worry.

There was no relief until you had hauled your gear over to the entrance of the tent, unzipped the front flap with unfeeling fingers, pulled out your mat and sleeping bag and a few odds and ends and thrust them into the tent. Jerry usually let me get in the tent first while he finished the staking I had started.

With numb paws, I rolled out the mat, straightened it

out on the icy floor, puffed up the sleeping bag, removed my icy boots, and crawled into the bag.

The task of stripping off my wet underwear in the cold was a shivering affair. I could always see the moisture of my breath and hear the snap of the wind. Then, with a new suit of underwear on—new only in the sense that I had not worn it that day—I'd crawl into the deep folds of the bag, pull the zipper shut above my head and lie still.

Slowly the cold would recede and the heat of my body became trapped by the down fluff of the bag. The warmth didn't come fast, but took time to settle in, rising within me. The first quarter hour I still shivered, but eventually the cold subsided and I began to bask in the warm bed.

Jerry always took longer. In fact, he couldn't get warm in his bag and had to go off to the mess tent for early soup, something extra to fill him with calories against the deep cold.

But I was warmed by the bag. That was all I needed—nothing more than a down bag to fill me with the warmth I yearned for. Soon I became satiated with heat. Gradually I dozed off until I heard the shout of *"Chow, Joe,"* awakening me from my warm nest. Then, I pulled on my jacket, jammed on my Canadian military boots, and crawled out into the cold white winter.

This, for 53 days, was my practice. But as we got closer and closer to the pole, the cold was growing deeper and more intense.

Our supplies were running low. We'd run through the regular meals and were now on emergency rations. Unless we had resupply, we would not be able to go on.

Plans were laid for Henry to make a drop in two days. He could make the drop only if the weather was clear in the Patriot Hills, the Thiels, and here—good conditions in all three places.

The next day was clear blue and the wind 5 to 10 miles per hour. The sastrugi were hard and rough, up to seven feet deep. It looked like a wild sea, the waves constantly shifting, sometimes curling under with deep holes in places that could catch you unaware.

It was tough sledding for the Ski-Doos, for the waves and swells could turn a sledge over and pitch it on its side.

To keep from falling on my face, I walked the entire day. The pain in my left leg was less, for the sedative kept it down.

The temperature had dropped to 9 degrees below zero. Again, we climbed the hard sastrugi, reaching 8,720 feet, a thousand feet higher than three days ago.

The snow formed long swells so that we kept rising and sinking. The sastrugi remained like a rough sea except for an hour in the afternoon, when the snow was soft.

After the first hour, I switched to walking, seeking the hard snow. I got so I could distinguish what was hard from what was soft by examining the flows and eddies of the surface. The high ridges were generally hard, as were the smooth surfaces and the regular eddies.

Sometimes a long smooth surface ran for a hundred yards where my boots would not sink. Following these surfaces meant angling off the direct line, but it was worth the effort because I avoided the soft snow, which was very tiring.

The snowmobile fuel was running low. Unless the Twin Otter could land soon, we would be stranded without food or water. But the terrain was too rough for bringing the airplane in. The holes in the sastrugi were extremely deep, too dangerous for the Twin Otter.

Martyn decided we must push on, and he sent Alejo ahead to find a safe place for the airplane to land.

But Shirley was having serious problems with her

foot. She had a huge blister and the bone had become extremely sore.

"I cannot ski beyond 7 o'clock," she insisted. "I can go no further."

It was already 7:00. Martyn looked perplexed. The landscape was a little smoother, but still rough.

"We should go further," said Alejo. "There is no place to land here."

Shirley wouldn't budge, however, so we decided to camp.

Martyn took charge of other matters: "Henry will be here tomorrow," he announced, "if the plane can land."

"Each tent should send out one personal duffel bag on the Otter and keep one bag," he said. "You will have to share a bag. If we do not do this, we will have too much weight for the plane to take off from the pole."

There were some groans and some statements of disbelief as to whether we could get everything we needed in one duffel bag.

"If there's too much," said Mike, "we'll just have to leave some things at the South Pole."

"Jim's worked out a list," continued Martyn. "You should have what's on the list but no more."

"These are the things you need to keep," Jim enumerated: "Extra long underwear, extra mitts, pile pants and jacket, down pants and jacket, Canadian military boots, and of course your Ensolite pad, your sleeping bag, and other normal equipment."

I decided not to keep my down pants. I'd already sent out the pile pants and jacket, though I'd kept a pile sweater. I could use my Thinsulite bib pants to serve the purpose of both the down and the pile pants and jacket.

Martyn finally decided that the Twin Otter could land near camp.

Martyn was on the radio: "Patriot Hills, Patriot Hills, Patriot Hills. This is Overland, Overland, Overland."

Henry answered the 10 o'clock call.

"Depart in 15 minutes," he reported. "The flight will take three hours and 15 minutes. We plan to stop in the Thiels for fuel resupply."

The receiver was kept on to monitor any calls. The weather was clear at Patriot Hills and here. The appearance of low clouds at either site or at the Thiels would force Henry to abort the flight. No one knew what the weather at the Thiels was like. Successful flight depended on a high ceiling at all three locations.

Around noon, Henry reported, "We made the Thiels depot," he radioed us. "But I can't find your markings! Where are they?"

"One kilometer west of the Lewis Nunatak," answered Jim.

The Lewis Nunatak was the last object to be seen between the Thiels and the South Pole. If Henry could not find the nunatak, he would never reach us.

There was a long silence. Then the radio cracked, "I can see eight kilometers of markings. But the cairns have fallen down." Henry reported.

"They're *tired,*" retorted Martyn.

I decided to retreat to my sleeping bag to make up for lost rest. The airfield has been laid out. It ran just west of camp, right through our tent. Markings had been placed to show the pilot where to set down. He would land just west of us in a southerly direction and slightly uphill.

Suddenly I was awakened by a shout. "You'll get a parking ticket unless you move your tent." It was Mike. "You've got two hours," he added.

I crawled out of the shelter, and Jerry and I picked up the tent and moved it 40 yards west. One other tent also had to be moved.

Our plan was quite simple. The Ski-Doos were to be left at the American South Pole Base, together with the sleds and sledges. They would be needed by Will Steger to move his food and equipment for his forthcoming trans-Antarctic expedition. Food and other supplies were also left at the South Pole for his use.

News of Henry's flight broke in periodically over the radio: *"Crevasses!* I see crevasses *right on your route.* Two or three miles long, wide and deep. I picked them up on radar."

Then the roar of the Twin Otter could be heard over the wind. We all rushed out to see.

Henry parked the plane 30 feet from our tent. Everyone grabbed sleds to haul the plastic food sacks from the plane. Henry refilled his engines with the aviation fuel he had stored in 50-gallon barrels in the plane.

Within an hour, all was ready for the plane to take off. We hugged Lise and said goodbye to Henry.

The Twin Otter rose slowly against the wind, circled once, and then headed north, away from the sun.

We had covered 600 miles and had only 150 miles to go. I could comprehend that distance. It was nearly the same as from my home in Minneapolis to Lake Superior.

I felt I could manage if my leg held out. The pain was less, but it was not gone. If the pain returned as before, *I might not make it.*

13 / ON THE POLAR PLATEAU

THE TEMPERATURE had dropped to 13 degrees below zero, reflecting the higher elevation. We were now at 9,000 feet above sea level.

I wore my usual suit: polypropylene long underpants and shirt, insulated suit with a Marmot jacket over it for added protection from the wind, a silk balaclava, pile hat, and Scott goggles and mask.

For the second day I switched from light to heavy polypropylene underwear to protect me from the lower temperatures of the Polar Plateau. On my feet, I wore tape, a single pair of polypropylene liner socks, and Merrill Telemark boots with insulated gaiters. I taped the bottom of the gaiters to cover the holes worn in them by walking in the snow.

The only change I had made since the early part of the

expedition had been to switch into heavy underwear from light underwear and to add the shell jacket. Because of the mask, I didn't need to wear sunscreen.

And because of the fog, I hadn't worn my prescription glasses for many weeks.

Ice, snow, and mountains—that was the scene that greeted the intruder into this barren land. At the land's edge of the continent, 80 degrees south and 80 degrees west, where we had begun our journey, we had been at about 400 feet above sea level.

We stood on a *cover of snow* at a depth measured in a varying number of feet. Below that was ice a *thousand feet* or more deep. Slowly, the shelf ice moved out to sea as the ice of the continent pushed downhill from the pole. At the continent's land edge, we were *9,000 feet below the pole*. The South Pole stood at an elevation of 9,300 feet *above* sea level.

To reach the pole we had to climb.

The climb was so gradual, 9,000 feet in 750 miles, that our rise was barely perceptible. We averaged only 18 feet per day, yet some days I imagined we climbed all day. The thought of eternal climbing was based on the fact that the sheet of ice was not perfectly flat, but moved in long swells, swells so long that it sometimes took a half a day or a day to pass from one crest in the ice to the next. In between the crest we rode the swell, descending downward to the trough, a very wide valley, and then up again against the next rise.

On the rise I felt the strain of the little red sled more and had to push harder on my poles, particularly when the rise was steep.

At least once every day I dreamed of arriving at the pole. Not that I consciously pictured it each time, but the image of reaching the goal flashed before me again and again.

I dreamed of seeing the South Pole station, of skiing slowly toward it and watching the members of the American station rush out to greet us. At times of euphoria, I envisioned our team being shown around the station and served a glorious meal of steak and potatoes.

I wanted the dream to come true, but I suspected it would not.

Sometimes I had other dreams about our arrival, dreams of a quite different sort. I dreamed that we were not greeted warmly, not made welcome, and even criticized for what we had done.

I knew that the National Science Foundation director of the American Antarctica program did not want us ·at the South Pole, did not want us to cross Antarctica by ski or in any other way. It had been made clear to Martyn they did not want him. They had pressured the Chilean government, over whose territory we travelled, not to allow us to make the trip.

The official reason for not welcoming us was that in case of emergency, the U.S. National Science Foundation would be forced to rescue us by sending an aircraft. Their skittishness on this score was understandable since they had once directed a foreign plane at McMurdo. The plane had crashed and the NSF had been sued by relatives of the survivors.

This was not the only official reason given. The other was that Antarctica was a dangerous place, not suited for tourists or other non-scientific travelers. Outsiders, it was further charged, polluted the pristine area.

The arguments, I felt, had little validity. Martyn had arranged his own means of rescue with his own DC-4 stationed in Punta Arenas, a Twin Otter stationed in the Patriot Hills, and a second Twin Otter stationed further down the peninsula.

In case of emergency, any of these planes was available to rescue us. Moreover, NSF, if asked for help, would bear no cost since it was their policy to charge for rescue.

As for polluting the environment, we carried all our garbage out. The National Science Foundation, in contrast, dumped all of theirs at the South Pole and at McMurdo where garbage, oil drums, and even large discarded airplanes were buried in the ice.

The NSF was a little like the stove calling the kettle black. They accused others of what they were guilty of.

It looked like the top officials of the NSF Antarctica program wanted to keep a continent the size of the United States for themselves—and keep everyone else out. This was despite the fact that the United States very graciously made no claims to the continent.

This view was expressed not only by the NSF, but by some of the scientists who did research. Some Antarctica scientists seemed to think that they were the only ones who had a right to be in the Antarctic. They disparaged explorations like ours.

This exclusivity seemed strange to me. Exploration of various kinds, including ours, had always been part of our tradition. Why should that right be restricted to a chosen few? Especially, since Antarctica has been little explored by foot.

As I traversed the snow moving south, I wondered who these people thought they were and why they thought the way they did.

Martyn had said that our plane would not be given permission to land on the base's snow runway. He had said that we would be given no official weather conditions when our plane departed for the pole.

Knowledge of such conditions could be very useful, of course, since knowing that the ceiling was too low to land could save fuel and money. The flight from Patriot Hills to the pole cost tens of thousands of dollars in fuel.

I gathered, however, that many of the actual people working at the pole were excited about our journey, anxious to see us and anxious to help. Marooned as they were for six months to a year, the diversion of our arrival would seem welcome.

As we got closer to the pole, I wondered about what sort of welcome we would receive.

On Christmas Eve, we had talked about calling the pole by radio.

Someone suggested sending Christmas greetings.

Mike was against doing so, but Martyn called anyway. There was no answer.

The station was on a different time schedule and our call reached the station early in the morning.

Later, however, we did begin to receive clandestine calls giving weather conditions.

Thus, we were in the strange position of being officially persona non grata, but receiving from station personnel information that would help our safety and facilitate our arrival.

Hugh Culver had notified the National Science Foundation in Washington of our impending arrival. As the last few days passed, and we got closer and closer to our goal, we made an official call to the station. We received the following reply:

"Your invitation is a foregone conclusion," he was told. "But, you come at your own risk."

To imply that our invitation was a "foregone conclusion," belied the NSF's attitude over the last three years. They hadn't wanted us to come. They had tried to stop us.

And, to say that we "come at our own risk," suggested

they did not know we had been at our own risk for two months. What an odd thing to say, I concluded.

The simple words: "you are welcome," would have been the normal reply.

But the NSF here was not normal. I had heard that here it was somewhat paranoid. The official message did little to dispel that opinion.

Even so, I was happy to hear anything from them.

I had dreamed so many times of our arrival at the U.S. South Pole station, I could only hope we would be truly welcome.

The whole day was clear until the last hour, when low clouds moved in from the northwest. The difficulty of the sastrugi varied from rough to quite easy. We covered 19 miles, and at this rate, Martyn predicted that we would reach the pole by January 17, one week away.

Our evening discussion of tactics was dominated by what we should do at the pole. Martyn wanted us to get in and out with as little fuss as possible. He outlined his view of the proper procedure:

"We should greet the station members when we arrive, but not fraternize with them. As soon as we have exchanged greetings, we can walk over to the symbolic South Pole for pictures and then go over to the real pole. We can move as a group. Then we can take any tour of the facility they offer. While we are doing that, Mike and Stuart will be able to prepare the sledges and Ski-Doos, which will be left for the Steger expedition. After we've done this we can depart for Patriot Hills."

"I think it's a good plan," I said, anxious to get home as soon as possible. Tori, Jerry, and Ron were also eager to fly out. Ron had used up two years' leave, Tori had school, and Jerry had business to attend to.

"We should stay 24 hours," said J.K. "This has been a long pilgrimage. It would be a shame to get to our goal and depart as soon as we got there."

Shirley wanted to stay for a much longer time. Shirley said we would get a full meal, not the usual donuts and coffee. I bet her that we would not.

Martyn noted that a letter from the Speaker of the House for special treatment had produced the usual two-hour official tour—and the usual donuts and coffee.

Mike, who had run a British Antarctic station for a year, cautioned us. "Remember that it is their home. We must act like guests."

With that, the discussion ended.

"We'll play it by ear," Martyn concluded.

Every day, Stuart and Mike attempted to fix our position accurately. They wanted to prevent any significant error in latitude. At this high southern latitude, a one percent error was one mile, which resulted in a one percent error in magnetic declination. That error could cause us to miss the South Pole.

We were skiing over the same snow we had skied over for nearly 500 miles—hard snow packed on 6,000 feet of ice. It was a surface that seemed as solid and secure as the Precambrian rock of the island of Manhattan.

The morning had been silent, the land undisturbed, when suddenly there was a sound we had not heard before, a sound that sent tremors through our spines.

It was a dull sound, a settling sound. It seemed to come from *everywhere*. It pervaded our entire world.

The snow under my skis shook in an unnerving tremor, as if in an earthquake. But it was not the earth that quaked, rather the great expanse of Antarctic snow underneath my feet.

Just as I began to recover from the fear of the unexpected sound, another great shock occurred. It seemed to radiate as far as I could see, as far as the distant horizon.

Crack! went the sound again. I could feel the snow below me settle, as if in great agony.

What was the sound? Was I in danger?

Frantically I searched my memory in an attempt to comprehend this terrifying experience, and I recalled similar shocks in the mountains of Canada. Only then the shocks had been the prelude to an avalanche.

My reaction in those situations had been to race to the shelter of the nearest stand of trees or protective rocks to avoid being buried alive by the snow. But here, there were no trees or rocks to shelter me. I could not find safety; there was no place to hide.

Then I heard someone shout, *"We're over crevasses!"*

But where were they?

So far, those we had crossed had been on the blue ice or steep hills. None had been on flat snow.

I knew that we had left our ropes behind and now lacked any means of tying ourselves together for protection. We could not prevent one another from falling into the deep fissures in the ice.

Although we had not known it, were on a narrow band of snow that bridged crevasses. We could not see the snow bridge or the hidden cracks in the ice.

We were like ants who thought the next nub of earth was a mountain; from this perspective we could not see or imagine the cracks in the earth, ready to devour us up.

"It's only snow settling," Martyn suggested. "Simply that, nothing more."

And we promptly dismissed the danger.

But the massive settling of snow continued through the next day, and the day after that and the day after that, prompting fear and uncertainty. We continued on, nonetheless, over snowfields that hid dangers we could not see—but could only guess at.

Each day, we heard the noise, and each day, we worried anew, perhaps without cause but just possibly with good reason.

"*Crevasses*," we now shouted to each other in harmless but nervous jest, "crevasses!" We were whistling in the dark, unsure of the danger we were in.

Only later did we discover the truth of the situation.

Only later did we see and finally understand.

The SATNAV had not worked since the 88th latitude when it had said we were at the equator. We were now dependent on our observations of the sun to know where we were.

We all knew that missing the pole completely and heading off toward the other side of the continent was a danger. Mike and Stuart were afraid that we might do just that unless we had very precise information on our location, particularly on our longitude.

The SATNAV was useless. Our hand sextant was too unsteady. Martin had rented a large Theodolite in Punta Arenas, had it flown to Patriot Hills in the DC-4, and had it sent on the second drop with Henry. Mike and Stuart took sun shots every hour while the rest of us were on the trail. Still, they debated with Martin about exactly where we were, and about how we knew where we were.

Martyn and Stuart still could not agree on how to determine our exact magnetic declination. By camp we were at 89 degrees south latitude. We had but one degree to go—69 miles left.

I was just about to start my meal when I looked at Tori. Her face was white, and she looked extremely ill.

Suddenly, she ran out of the tent, unable to finish her food.

"Food poisoning?" I asked.

"Carbon monoxide," Jim answered.

"What caused it?" someone asked

"The *stoves,*" Jim said. "She spent too much time up near the stoves. As soon as she gets some air, she'll be okay."

At 89 degrees, 35 seconds south, we were only 25 nautical miles to the pole, which we expected to reach in two days. By coincidence, that date of January 17 was the same day in history that Scott had reached the South Pole.

For safety purposes, we had been asked to report our location to the South Pole station. Clearly the head of the station was concerned about risk—not ours, but *theirs.*

They need not have worried.

"I think we will get a good reception," J.K. said.

14 / END OF THE
JOURNEY

THE HOURS, DAYS, AND WEEKS of the
expedition merged into one. My past fears slowly
subsided into an overwhelming anticipation. I forgot
my early anxieties that I might not be accepted, that I
had not trained enough, that my body could stand the
toil, or that I could take the mental anguish.

My fantasies of reaching the South Pole now seemed
close to reality.

The final day dawned mostly clear, with only
scattered clouds. The snow conditions were excellent,
with two inches of powder, with no sastrugi.

We set off in single file, skiing uphill in the snow. We
plugged on, each of us absorbed in his or her own

thoughts. For the first time, the snowmobiles joined our march.

I heard a sudden roar above me. Thinking it must be a National Science Foundation plane, I swung around, looked up, and saw our Twin Otter buzzing us. Henry circled once and then headed off toward the South Pole, disappearing in the distance.

T oward noon, I heard someone ahead of me shout: *"I can see the buildings."*

I couldn't see anything yet. Much as I wanted to hurry, I could not.

"People," Ron shouted. *"They're waiting, watching."*

Then the bodies began to appear in my vision—a line of figures, which gradually lengthened.

"I *see* them!" I yelled at last.

W e stopped, then hugged each other as we came near the pole.

"Let's form a line," Stuart said.

We formed a single line, perpendicular to our line of march.

"Formation right," shouted J.K., trying to give us a more uniform position, as we moved in a broad front toward our destination.

I n the distance, I could see the waiting line grow larger, the crowd waiting.

The onlookers waved at us.

Tears came into my eyes. We waved in return.

I felt an enormous sense of relief. Until now, I had never been sure that I would make it.

Now it seemed almost unreal.

"Congratulations," I heard as I approached.

"Great job. Well done."

Then came the rapid flow of questions:

"Did you ski the whole way?" "What equipment did

you take?" "How did the group get along with one another?" "What was it like skiing?"

There were many questions. I tried to answer each as best I could.

I was so happy I could barely talk.

After a time, Martyn said, "We should get on with what we have to do."

So we walked our last paces toward the geographic South Pole.

Then we stood there, in awe.

We were at the very bottom of the world. The mystical South Pole.

The end of the earth.

What happened after that was anticlimactic. Now that we had achieved our objective, we were invited to examine the large base.

It was the *official tour.* We crossed the 10,000-foot runway, a snow-packed surface kept cleared by enormous bulldozers.

Before us rose the dome itself, an aluminum structure 55 feet high and 165 feet wide. It had two tunnel openings, one on each side, and was partly covered with snow. Inside were a half-dozen insulated structures that rested on the snow floor of the great dome.

To our right, I could see the Quonset-like structures that housed the summer staff of 80 or so. In the winter, there were only 20 or 30 persons here at the base. Further to the right, I saw the science dome and beyond that a variety of yellow snow-moving equipment.

We visited the station mess—for the *official* donuts and coffee.

Shirley had lost her bet about the full meal deal of steak and potatoes.

The assistant base commander, an employee of ITT, which ran the base, described the facilities and gave us the tour. J.K. made a short and quite touching speech and presented his country's flag. We listened to a description of the scientific work carried out by the scientists at the base and saw the buildings housing the science lab, the medical center, and the heating plant.

We learned a little more about the terrain we had crossed. As we had neared the pole itself, we found we were skiing on only about an inch of snow.

The personnel at Amundsen-Scott base had joked, "You must have had great skiing—a two-mile base and an inch of powder."

Now our concern turned to getting out. The timetable was tight. The DC-4 was to have come in from Punta Arenas to our distant base camp and be waiting for us when we flew the Twin Otter out of here.

"Will the DC-4 get there?" I asked Henry.

"It *should*," he answered in his shorthand way.

"What about *us*?"

"*If* we can get off within the half hour. The weather is closing in"

If we didn't get off quickly, we wouldn't reach Patriot Hills in time.

"The DC-4 can lay over only four hours," Henry added. "Otherwise its engines become too cold to start."

So we had to move quickly, or we would never meet the DC-4. If we tarried too long, it could be another week before conditions were good enough for another try.

Most of us were milling about, ready to go. Henry looked anxious. Jerry and I were the two most eager to move off.

But as we waited, I saw Shirley turn her back on us and begin walking away.

"What's she *up to?*" I asked.

"Who *knows!*" Jerry replied, hunching his shoulders.

To my amazement, I watched her stop and begin to *take off* her heavy down parka. Then her jacket, next her boots, and after that her pants.

What is going on? I wondered with alarm.

Then it dawned on me: Shirley had said she that if she got to the South Pole, she planned to strip down to her Christian Dior panties and bra.

I hadn't taken her remarks seriously. No one had.

Slowly, she pulled off her long-underwear tops, then the bottoms. The ten of us, the reporter from *National Geographic,* and the pole station personnel looked on.

"She's down to her *skivvys,*" someone said. It was like a cold-weather strip tease—at 18 degrees below.

Why was she doing this? I scratched my beard in amazement, recalling the words of a former South Pole commander: "There are three kinds of people who go to the Antarctic: boy scouts, egocentrics, and egomaniacs"

Soon I saw someone pick up a video camera and begin filming her standing in her Christian Dior panties and bra in the sub-zero weather.

The unreal show seemed to take nearly an hour, delaying us. I was certain we would not make our DC-4 connecting flight.

The sky began to cloud as we took off and grew increasingly thick as the Twin Otter flew north. We followed our tracks all the way to the Thiels, flying quite low.

I had imagined getting on this plane so many times that it now seemed to be an anticlimax. The unreality of it all continued.

There were still real problems ahead. If we reached the DC-4 in Patriot Hills on time, we could land in

Chile tomorrow. That was not very likely, however, since we had tarried so long at the South Pole.

The DC-4 could not remain in the Antarctic more than four hours, or its engines would be too cold to start. Unless we got there soon, it would have to return to Punta Arenas and come back later when the weather was favorable.

As we traveled north toward the Thiels, I watched the snow sweep by under the wings of our plane. The sun was in the east now, and so visibility on my side of the plane was good. The snow below sparkled under the slanting rays of sunshine.

Soon, clouds began to billow in, and I lost sight of the Antarctic surface below. And I tried to forget.

"Crevasses!" someone exclaimed, "crevasses below!"

To my horror, I saw deep crevasses stretching in long lines below us. There were two sets of crevasses, one on each side of a narrow path of snow that ran between them.

The truth dawned on me.

That narrow snow bridge unwittingly had been *our* path.

By some miracle, we had gone *between* the two sets of crevasses, somehow missing both. Our escaping them had been just plain dumb luck.

But our problems were not over. Henry had left a cache of fuel that was needed to make the second leg of the journey from the pole to Patriot Hills. Despite our having shipped out everything not needed in order to lighten the plane, we had only enough gas to make the fuel cache in the Thiel Mountains.

As we approached the Thiels, I heard Jim say: "There's King Peak—and the snow ramp we climbed."

"The fuel cache is 20 miles beyond."

As we bumped our way north toward the fuel, clouds

closed in. The plane jolted about like a top in the high wind. I cinched in my seat belt.

"Socked in," someone said.

With a sinking feeling, I peered through the window, I saw only dense clouds. Would we be able to land at all?

Miraculously, a brief opening appeared in the mist and King Peak and the ice below became visible.

Henry circled the blue ice and throttled back into the wind. I could see the ice coming up to meet us; I felt the skis bounce on the rough surface and then the shudder of the plane as it slowly came to a stop.

Henry's face appeared in the doorway.

"Camping time again!" he announced. *"Can't make the fuel dump."*

The DC-4 would return to Punta Arenas, a ten-hour flight. We would be stranded here for who knows how long. Nearly all our food was gone.

When the back door of the plane was opened, a blast of air rushed in. The wind had risen to 40 miles per hour and snow was being driven north.

We grabbed the tents, sleeping bags, and shovels, and climbed down into the wind to set up camp. The mess tent had been left at the South Pole for Steger, so we had no mess tent and not much food.

After erecting the other tents, we built large snow walls to the windward side of each. We cut other snowblocks to lay on the snow flaps of the tents; the snow was not soft enough to be shoveled over the flaps. When the camp was complete, it looked like a fortress, with a long snow wall serving as a barrier to our natural enemy, the wind.

Once our tents were up and fortified, I crawled into our tent, unpacked my sleeping bag, and got in. My internal clock was completely askew.

The South Pole was on New Zealand time, Patriot

Hills on Chilean time, and we, on our own time, quite different than the other two. In terms of our own time schedule, we were well into the early hours of the morning, but the sun gave no sign of this.

I fell asleep immediately, wondering how long we might be imprisoned here. It could be a day, a week, or even longer.

But the rising force of the storm, and the disappearance of King Peak in the clouds, suggested that we would be here some time.

I slept for 24 hours, rising from my deep slumber only for food, soup, chocolate, and on one occasion, spaghetti. In the main, we were all hibernating, holed up against the storm.

When the wind let up for a time, Martyn and Stuart hiked down to the blue ice field just south of camp.

As the hours passed, I lost all sense of time. We were trapped here by the wind and clouds. Fuel was 20 miles to the north, a day away by ski. But we had no sleds with which to haul the fuel back, even if we did get to it.

There was no chance of escape until the ceiling lifted. How long that would be, no one knew.

The wind continued to beat against the walls of the tent, and the snow drifts rose steadily.

After a day of immersion in my bag, I came to and began to think of home. I wondered when I might return.

I dozed off and on, and on the last awakening, I crawled out of my tent into the clear, cold weather. It had stopped snowing. I could see the blue ice in the distance and, beyond the ice, King Peak.

The ceiling to the north had risen. It almost seemed clear enough to fly north, possibly clear enough to reach the fuel depot.

I overheard Henry's radio call.

"Patriot Hills, Patriot Hills, Patriot Hills. This is Bravo, Bravo, Bravo. Over."

There was a long silence before I heard Henry's disgusted reply.

"Back to the drawing board."

The weather here was flyable. The weather in Patriot Hills was not.

I could only return to my tent, wondering when and if we would get out, stuck as we were halfway between the South Pole and Patriot Hills.

I dozed off for another two hours and was abruptly awakened by Martyn's words: *"We're flying in half an hour."*

Jerry and I crawled out of our sleeping bags. Thrilled at the prospect of departure, we dressed immediately and packed our gear.

Outside, the engines of the Twin Otter turned over and soon roared, as the plane taxied out and took off for the north. Henry had gone to refuel.

Hopefully, he could land at the depot

Jim brought lukewarm instant coffee and cookies. I pulled on my heavy boots and parka and crawled out of the tent into the cold wind. I lifted the snow blocks off the tent, and, as soon as Jerry emerged, pulled the stakes and began to remove the tent poles. Soon all the tents had been struck, stuffed in their bags, and lined up with the duffels.

The Twin Otter returned within a half hour, circled, landed into the wind, and then taxied to camp. Henry loaded the duffels we handed him on the right side of the plane and placed the skis under the seat before we boarded.

Slowly, the plane taxied back on the ice, turned toward the mountains and lifted off.

At last, we were on the final leg to base camp. I

relaxed, as I had not relaxed before, knowing that once we reached Patriot Hills, we would be secure from danger with plenty of food and water. From there, we had but one more flight to go to return to civilization.

We crossed down the valley between the Ellsworth Mountains and the Patriot Hills, the valley we had skied two months ago, passed over the snow saddle we had climbed, banked toward base camp, and finally landed on the blue ice. We were back to our starting point.

We were almost home. We still had to wait for the DC-4 to meet us, if the wind was not too high or the ceiling too low.

Lise had a buffet luncheon waiting when we reached the mess tent. There was fruit, sandwich meat, bread, cakes—everything we could want. We ate to our heart's content. This pleasure was overshadowed, though, by the news that the DC-4 was on its way.

Morton arrived on the plane with three cameras dangling from his shoulders and began taking photos as soon as he saw us. He immediately poured out a stream of news. Leo had been sick and could not come.

Lise and Henry would remain in the Patriot Hills for a few more weeks to complete the caches for Steger's trans-Antarctic expedition. Mike Sharp planned to stay with them. Gordon Wiltsie's ski tour had been plagued by two weeks of whiteout. The equipment we had left at base camp had been sent to Punta Arenas on the earlier flight.

We were all anxious to get started. The aircraft had been refueled and the sky was clear, perfect for taking off. When word came that it was time to board. J.K. and I started off together, trekking the last yards we would cover in the Antarctic.

We had just buckled down when one of the engines failed to start. The plane mechanic climbed out of the plane, down an aluminum ladder. In a moment, I saw his head disappear into the cowl of the engine, just beyond the propeller.

I began worrying again, recalling that this plane had been beset by mechanical problems last year. My fears were unfounded. The mechanic returned; the engines started. Soon, we wheeled into position, taxied north toward camp, turned, and accelerated south over the ice toward Patriot Hills. Mike, Lise, and Henry waved as we lifted off.

Within a few minutes, we had turned north for Punta Arenas.

I took my first sleeping pill of the trip for the 10-hour flight, but, with the excitement of returning, I still could not sleep at first. I finally drifted off and awoke just as the plane banked into Punta Arenas and landed on the hard runway. The sight of green fields for the first time in months was a wonder to behold.

Upon our return, not only were we welcomed by a full press conference, with reporters from as far away as Santiago, but we were treated to upgraded lodging. We found ourselves escorted to a much classier hotel.

For me, the prize I had so longed for and dreamed of over these many weeks, was the simple but wonderful prospect of taking a bath—a hot, steaming bath. Over the past weeks, I had planned out the sequence of events on my return to Punta Arenas in precise detail.

Within a minute of my arrival in my warm hotel room, I proceeded to the bathroom and eyed with appreciation the electric lights, running water, toilet, and bath tub. I stripped off the clothes that had lasted two months' wear, bundled the outer garments into a clothes bag for later cleaning, and discarded the underwear into the waste basket for immediate burning. I looked at my gaunt body: I was to learn later that I had lost 35 pounds.

Then, having filled the tub with hot, steaming water, I entered the precious substance.

Savoring the experience, I slipped beneath the warm liquid all the way up to my neck, and lay in ecstasy for the better part of an hour. I relished every minute of it, soaping and resoaping myself to remove two months' grit.

Next, I placed a call to Diana. She was home when I called. It was wonderful to talk to her, but she had some disturbing news.

"You won't be home when I arrive?" I repeated. *"In Arizona?"* I repeated again.

Diana would be visiting her father when I returned, much to my dismay. "I'll come to Arizona," I ended.

Next, the ice cream sundae. We met in the lobby, Ron, Tori, and I, and proceeded immediately to a bar and soda restaurant.

"Ice cream sundae!" I instantly ordered, hoping the Spanish-speaking waitress would understand. She did, and soon, the inside of my mouth burned from gulping down the creamy delicacy too fast.

That night came the banquet, a formal, many-course affair held at the private club on Magellan Square. Everyone here was connected in some way with the expedition, from the pilot of the plane to Jerry's and Alejo's wives.

Hugh Culver gave a speech with gracious compliments to Leo LeBon, smoothing over past disputes. J.K. and Martyn gave a few farewell remarks as well. It was a touching event.

I gazed up through the glass-roofed dining room, where the stars of the southern hemisphere could be seen. I suddenly realized that this was the first time in two months that I had seen the stars.

After I returned to the hotel, I spent most of the next two days in bed. Ironically, I had to recover not from my Antarctic adventure—but from stomach poisoning I had contracted while in this city.

Then I boarded the Lan Chile flight to Miami to fly directly home.

As the long passage began, memories of the remarkable trip flooded back—the longest journey by foot that I probably would ever take. I thought about the planning, the training in Washington and the Yukon, and finally, the months of ordeal over the Antarctic ice.

The expedition had tested us all in many ways: physically, mentally, psychologically, and emotionally. Although I couldn't be certain of exactly what achieving this goal meant to every individual, I knew it was deeply felt by each of us. Especially me.

We had crossed several significant mileposts: we were the first Americans to reach the South Pole overland by ski. Tori and Shirley were the first women to make it. As an expedition, we were the fourth, but our accomplishment as a team was to pioneer a new route and make it navigable.

We had endured the sun, the wind, the cold, and had completed the effort. We were not professional, hardened athletes, backed by millions in corporate financing and promotion, but were amateur adventurers who primarily had done the journey for the love of adventure.

We had skied to the end of the earth, stood together at the South Pole, and we had emerged as companions and friends.

And we had renewed our faith with our increasingly fragile and remote environment—even its most hostile region.

As I write this, my skis are standing in a corner of my den. I look at the fresh snow outside the window and then at the skis.

A faint thought crossed my mind.

No, not again this year, I admonished myself. In fact, *not for a while.* But skiing was starting to appeal to me again.

The telephone rang. It was a friend of mine.

"Want to join us for a weekend over in Wisconsin?"

I asked him what he intended to do, somewhat suspiciously.

I knew him. He was a humorist.

"Cross-country ski!" he burst out, gleefully.

I was amused. But on a scale of one to ten, I had to tell him his wonderful suggestion rated a below zero.

Way below zero.

That firmly settled, I settled back in my easy chair, pulled out some more travel brochures, and began to dream of spring.

E P I L O G U E

Not long after the expedition, Jerry Corr flew to the North Pole with Henry Perk.

Later, Martyn Williams and Jerry started at the South Pole and skied four hundred miles along Robert Falcon Scott's original route to the Ross Ice Shelf, carrying their own gear. After that, they planned to attempt Mount Everest from Nepal.

Alejo has similar plans.

Mike Sharpe and Shirley Metz practiced navigation out of Patriot Hills. Mike then headed north to Canada to ski down Elsworth Island.

Shirley lectured on Society Expedition tours in Antarctica, showed her videos to audiences in the United States, and visited Paris to participate in Antarctica treaty talks.

J.K. returned to India to the Mountaineering School. Ron Milnarik went helicopter skiing in Canada.

Regrettably, Giles Kershaw, the pilot we met in Patriot Hills, was killed while flying in Antarctica.

Reinette Senum, having missed out on the expedition, organized her own, the 1991 Woman's Transantarctic Expedition. She will co-lead it with Ann Bancroft, who was a member of the Steger North Pole Expedition.

Will Steger and his International Trans-Antarctica

Expedition completed its dog sled trek across Antarctica, using some of the supplies we had left.

Tori Murden returned to Louisville, Jim Williams to Wyoming, and Stuart Hamilton to the Yukon.

Of the others, I have not heard. I got a desk job in Minneapolis, which precluded my Annapurna plans, but it allowed me to spend two weeks windsurfing in Hawaii, where it was *warm*.

APPENDIX A

GROUP EQUIPMENT

Tents and cooking

Group cook and mess tent
Cooking gear and stoves
Four-person tents

Motor transport

2 Ski-Doos
2 large sleds
Ski-Doo gas drums
Ski-Doo spare parts
Ski-Doo repair kits

Communications

100-watt HF radio
Solar panel
Antennae and mast
Backup 10 watt HF radio
ARGUS system satellite
locator beacon and
message transmitter

In-group communications

11 VHF locators
Transmitters
11 VHF radios
2 VHF tracking receivers

Directional instruments

Magnetic compass
Sun compass
SATNAV receiver
Sextant
Sled wheel

Weather recording instruments

Thermometer
Wind meter
Altimeter

Safety

Climbing ropes
Climbing gear
First aid kits
Ski repair kit
Sewing kit
Wax kit
General repair kit

PERSONAL EQUIPMENT LIST

Sleeping bags, rated to
-40 degrees F
Closed cell foam sleeping
pads
Vapor barrier socks
2 sets socks
2 sets long underwear,
polypropylene type
1 set pile jacket and pants
1 extra pile jacket

1 warm down or polar-
guard jacket
1 warm down or polar-
guard pants
1 wind jacket
1 wind pants
3 sets mitts: 1 regular , 1
overmitts, 1 spare regular
2 hats: 1 balaclava heavy
or fleece-lined, 1 ski-type
hat
1 balaclava lightweight
1 face mask
1 pair of overboots
1 set camp boots
(Canadian military boots)
1 large pack
1 duffel bag
1 ice axe
6 carabiners
40 foot 6 mm. rope
1 body harness
1 jumar
1 pulley
1 ice screw
1 sun screen
1 lip screen
1 zinc oxide
2 sets sunglasses
1 pair ski goggles with
face mask
1 1-liter water bottle
1 thermos bottle
1 Swiss army knife
1 two-cup measuring cup
1 pee bottle (small water
bottle)

1 compass
1 set metal edged skis,
waxable
1 set of skins
1 set of crampons
1 set lightweight skis,
waxable
1 set adjustable xc poles
1 toilet kit
camera and film
1 shovel
1 snow saw
1 pair double boots,
telemark
1 pair lightweight
racing boots
1 pair stiff skating skis
1 pair overboot for racing
boots

Other

Reading materials
Writing materials
Listening tapes

SUPPORT SERVICES

Aircraft Flights & Support

Twin Otter

--Three flights to Ronn
Ice Shelf
--Fuel Cache at Thiel
Mountains -85 degrees
--Flights from South Pole

to Patriot Hills for group egress at the end of the expedition.

DC-4

--Delivery of passengers to Patriot Hills from Punta Arenas
--DC.4 delivery of fuel to Patriot Hills
--Delivery of passengers to King George Island (or by Twin Otter)
--Delivery of equipment to Patriot Hills

EQUIPMENT AND SUPPORT SERVICES

Equipment & food

2 snowmobiles, plus one spare snowmobile - heavy duty design

Mobile radio equipment for the expedition

Base camp radio equipment for Patriot Hills

Fuel for snowmobiles for 900 miles

Spare parts and repair equipment for snowmobiles

Skiing equipment for trip

Miscellaneous equipment and supplies for caches

Miscellaneous equipment for trip

Food for 60 days

GUIDES AND SUPPORT STAFF:

Trip leader / guide / cook

Assistant / guide / cook,

2 snowmobile drivers/ mechanics / guides/ cooks

Radio operator and logistics person at the Patriot Hills base on 24- hour contact basis

Additional back-up rescue support of Chilean Air Force

Liaison person in Punta Arenas on 24-hour contact basis, with FAX, Telex and telephone

Twin Otter aircraft based at 80 degrees south for emergency use

PRELIMINARY
LOGISTICS AND
WEIGHTS

Equipment to be moved between resupply points located every two degrees of latitude—every 132 miles:

4 four person tents, 60 lbs.

Large cookshelter/ sleeping tent, 60 lbs.

2 HF radios, 20 lbs.

Misc. group equipment, 100 lbs.

Food for 15 days, 525 lbs.

Fuel for 15 days, 60 lbs.

Subtotal: 1,025 lbs.

Gas for snowmobiles, 600 lbs.
2 sleds, 300 lbs.

Total load being towed: 1,925 lbs

Personal equipment at 40 lbs x 11 = 440 lbs

INDEX

A

Adventure Network, *20, 21, 28, 30, 43*
Annapurna, *13*
Australian Geographic, 99

B

Bacteria, *159*
Baggage, *52, 55, 57, 65, 78*
Bhutan, *15*
Birds, *54, 160, 161*
Bivouac, *66, 77, 78, 87, 131*
Blisters, *55, 145*
Blue ice, *73, 100, 101, 107, 108, 109, 110, 121, 138, 139, 141, 175, 184, 187*
Boots, *54, 66, 104, 168*
British Antarctic, *59, 174*
Broken collar bone, *6, 35, 36, 45, 67, 113*
Bugaboos, *45*
Byrd, Admiral, *12*

C

Camera, *66, 67, 80, 82, 92, 146, 182, 187*
Canadian Mountain Holiday, *77, 121*
Chile, *45, 54, 57, 79, 183, 190*

C (continued)

Chilian government, *4, 42, 170*
Christmas, *17, 104, 127-136*
Clothing, *23, 58, 62, 118*
Cold weather, *135*
Crevasse, *13, 19, 27, 33, 34, 40, 60, 61, 71, 106, 138-141, 156, 175, 176, 183*

D

DC-4, *25, 68-70, 76, 101, 176, 181-184*
Dawson Creek, *38*
Drake Passage, *69*

E

Ellsworth Mountains, *71, 81, 91, 93, 96, 101, 106-107*
Equipment, *14, 19, 24, 27, 29, 30, 41, 43, 49, 50, 54, 58, 61, 75, 77, 118, 125, 140, 147, 151, 165, 167, 179, 180, 187*

F

Food, *13, 26, 39, 40, 58, 78-85, 118, 120-126, 139, 149, 156, 164, 167, 176, 184-187*
Frostbite, *11, 116, 159*

S

T

Martin